Eating Well Made Easy

Lorraine Pascale

Eating Well Made Easy

Deliciously healthy recipes
for everyone, every day

HarperCollins

Photography by Myles New

To my mum. Thank you for inspiring me to always believe that
I can do whatever I put my mind to ... Love and God bless.

HarperCollins*Publishers*
1 London Bridge Street
London SE1 9GF

www.harpercollins.co.uk

First published by HarperCollins*Publishers* 2015

10 9 8 7 6 5 4 3 2

Text © Lorraine Pascale 2015
Photography © Myles New 2015

Lorraine Pascale asserts the moral right to be identified as the
author of this work

A catalogue record of this book is available from the British Library

HB ISBN: 978-0-00-748970-1
EB ISBN: 978-0-00-748971-8

Food styling: Marina Filippelli
Props styling: Liz Belton

Printed and bound in Italy by L.E.G.O. SpA.

MIX
Paper from
responsible sources

FSC
www.fsc.org

FSC™ C007454

FSC™ is a non-profit international organisation established to promote the
responsible management of the world's forests. Products carrying the FSC
label are independently certified to assure consumers that they come from
forests that are managed to meet the social, economic and ecological needs
of present and future generations, and other controlled sources.

eating well
made easy

The essence of this book is tasty food. Tasty family food that is quietly healthy. By quietly healthy I mean still your favourite recipes, which you love and enjoy, but with bits of the recipe adjusted here and there, be it by cooking method or by ingredients, to make the recipes better for you.

There are lots of fabulous recipe books out there, many extolling the virtues of goji berries, chia seeds and other mystical ingredients, but if you are a busy mum/girlfriend/student/ (insert other here …) like me, when you come in from work you just want dishes that are fast, easy, accessible and tasty. As this book was originally due to come out in the winter, I also wanted to make sure it had a warm and cosy feel. There are salads and lighter foods in here, of course, which are great for things like lunches and snacks, but healthy comfort food was my goal. Food that still wraps you up from the inside out and makes everything feel like 'home'. Or at least your imagined idyll of what home should taste like. Those of you who know a bit about me will know that I like to learn a lot, to study a lot and to always find ways of improving myself. Whether those goals are ever reached in a way that will allow me to slow down a bit is still an unanswered question …

But I do love at least to try seeking out new information to enhance whatever I am doing. Recently I started to get into fitness, health, exercise and things of that nature. I fell in love with it all and really wanted to find a way to mix it up with what I was doing and known for (mainly making cakes!).

At the start of my real enjoyment of fitness I had a cake shop in Covent Garden, but the lease had just come up for renewal and the rent had increased three-fold. I loved the girls who worked in there, I loved the location of the shop, I loved the memories of what it took to get it up and running and, of course, I loved the cakes. However, the new rent would be crippling. On top of this was the knowledge of the new path I wished to take – health and fitness – and how I wanted to make people feel better about themselves. Of course, I still eat, cook and write recipes for cake, but it felt like the road of the cupcake business had come to an end for me and we made the sad decision to close the shop down.

I then began Instagramming healthy recipes like mad – developing them, cooking them, eating them and writing about them – and although the memory of my cupcake shop is often on my mind, I know I made the right decision to close it down. But still to this day, several months on, I have not visited Covent Garden again … I am not quite ready yet.

This may feel like a digression from the point of why I am writing this book, but it was important for me to tell you how I made the jump from cakes to healthy comfort food. I am now halfway through a nutritional diploma from the Institute for Integrative Nutrition. I had started doing a masters degree in nutrition, but after starting lessons I realised it wasn't quite for me. So I began researching courses that really got my heart racing, that were steeped in new findings and confronted head-on the multifaceted and often confusing world of nutrition. And I'm loving the studying I have been doing.

There are so many diet books on the market, which means, of course, so many diet-book authors! Yes, I am tall and yes, I appear slim, but I have also had my struggles with diet. During my pregnancy with my daughter I piled on 4 stone, and while modelling I became bulimic for a few months. Whether you are a size 6 or a size 16, if your clothes start to become too tight and uncomfortable and you are having to buy bigger sizes due to your style of eating, the discomfort and inner feelings of shame, guilt, disappointment and despair are present in many of us. I found that when I started thinking about my food as a way of life rather than a way to get thin, a safety valve inside me was released and I relaxed into enjoying food more. Of course, there have been times when there is a beach holiday coming up or a special occasion when I have upped my vegetables and perhaps eaten more lean chicken and fish. However, for the day to day, just having some simple guidelines to follow has made my relationship with food a more pleasurable one.

I am asked so often about healthy eating, how people can lose weight and what is the best thing for them to do for X, Y and Z with their food. Each diet has its place and I would not speak out of turn to judge them in any way; however, I struggle with the idea that one diet can suit all. We all like and dislike different things, our genes dictate so much and our bodies react differently to everything, so a one-size-fits-all 'diet' is a tough ask. That's why I have created a book that contains recipes for everyone. Whether you want to go dairy-free, gluten-free, meat-free or raw, you will find recipes here to suit your needs. I can only tell you what I have been learning and what I do in my life, and hopefully something will resonate with you that makes sense and makes you think you might choose to do it too.

Here are a few of the healthy guidelines that I am following, which have helped me feel healthier and happier:

I have discovered the benefits of eating SIRTfoods

I have been working with nutritionists Glen Matten and Aidan Goggins, and they introduced me to the study of SIRTfood. SIRTfoods are a selection of everyday foods that are naturally high in chemicals that activate powerful enzymes in the body, which are vital for many important biological processes. These foods are known as sirtuin activators. The study of SIRTfoods is still very new, but it is now thought that the chemicals in some foods activate the sirtuin enzymes to contribute to a wide range of health benefits including burning fat, reducing appetite, building muscle and improving the memory. In other words, they are amazing!

Some of the plants we eat are packed with sirtuin activators and some contain very little. Those foods considered to be SIRTfoods include green tea, dark chocolate, turmeric, kale, blueberries, parsley, citrus fruits, apples and onions. But don't worry, this doesn't limit your diet to just these foods. What I love about the SIRTfood approach is that you can still eat a healthy and varied diet of fresh fruit, veg, meat and fish, but simply top up with SIRTfoods. How easy is that?

Follow the guidelines on the opposite page to ensure you are getting the right amounts of these amazing SIRTfoods and revolutionise your health:

SIRTfoods

SIRTfood	Serving Size	Recommended Intake
Kale Rocket (wild) Watercress Pak Choi Chinese cabbage Radish leaves (raw) Olives Onions (white, red, spring)	One large full handful	2+ servings per day
Green tea	One green tea teabag or ¼ teaspoon of matcha green tea	3 servings per day
Dark chocolate (85% cocoa solids)	15g	1–2 servings per day
Herbs and spices (parsley, dill, coriander, thyme, oregano, cinnamon, turmeric)	Use liberally in meal preparation every day	
Capers	Use liberally in meal preparation every day	
Chillies (green, red, Jalapeño, Bird's eye, Habanero, etc.)	Use liberally in meal preparation every day	
Berries	100g	1 serving per day
Natural soy (miso, tempeh, tofu and nattō)	50g	1–2 servings per week

Immune Boosts

A strong immune system is the cornerstone of health, keeping our bodies in tip-top condition and those nasty colds and bugs at bay. Frequent consumption of medicinal mushrooms, such as shiitake and oyster, for example, is a great way of boosting our immune system, as is encouraging a favourable balance of gut-friendly bacteria in our diets. The right balance of prebiotics (substances found in certain vegetables that make the pre-existing good bacteria in the gut healthier) and probiotics (cultures containing good bacteria found in foods such as yoghurt) helps to prime the immune system and keep it functioning well – which all sounds very friendly indeed!

Immune Boost foods

Immune Boost	Active Nutrient	Serving Size	Recommended Intake
Medicinal mushrooms (shiitake and oyster)	Immune regulating polysaccharides	50g	2 servings per week
Chicory root	Prebiotic Fibre	10g	1 serving per day
Jerusalem artichokes	Prebiotic Fibre	20g	1 serving per day
Asparagus	Prebiotic Fibre	120g	1 serving per day
Sauerkraut	Probiotics	2 tbsp	2 servings per week
Garlic	Allicin	Use liberally in cooking and dressings	

I'm enjoying the benefits of some amazing foods

I wanted to make sure I included ingredients in this book that perform best in terms of nutritional benefits, but are also relatively easy to get hold of in your local supermarket and easy on your purse. These are some of my favourites …

I have used berries a great deal in smoothies, breakfasts, brunches and sweets, as they contain polyphenols, which help make them a slow energy releaser. Specifically, blueberries are a rich source of anthocyanins which are said to be good for the heart and may help reduce the risk of developing diabetes as we age.

Now I know Brussels sprouts are not everyone's favourite; however, they are packed full of vitamins and minerals as well as anti-cancer compounds called isothiocyanates – so we should eat them more often! Try my Shaved Raw Brussels Sprout Salad with Hazelnuts, Pomegranates and Pumpkin Seeds (see page 194).

Tomatoes are full of lycopene, which is known to prevent heart disease and is a powerful antioxidant, that may help protect cells from damage. Tomatoes are more nutritious once they have been cooked for a short time. Try my Roast Red Pepper, Tomato and Caramelised Onion Soup with Buckwheat (see page 68).

Sweet potato, pumpkin and butternut squash are three of my favourite veg and are great alternatives to starchy white potatoes. Carotenoids give these vegetables their strong colour and are great for boosting eye health.

Cocoa has the highest available source of flavanols, which boost heart and brain health – so a great reason to try my Chocolate, Banana and Ginger Super-Quick Mousse (see page 284).

Garlic has a host of nutritional benefits: it is a strong immune and cardiovascular booster and a natural antibiotic – it should be used as much as possible! Similarly, onions and shallots are another great food to incorporate into your daily cooking. They are rich in flavonoids, which are mostly concentrated in the outer layers of the vegetable, so try to remove as little of these as possible.

Capers are the food highest in quercetin, a plant compound with strong antioxidant and anti-inflammatory effects, which may help to protect against heart disease and cancers.

Eggs are a rich source of protein – great for days when you are eating less meat. I like to have eggs first thing in the morning as the protein keeps me full right up until lunch.

So I am trying to incorporate these amazing foods into my diet as much as possible … I do not always get it on point every day, but I do give it a go!

Red meat

I think red meat should be eaten only in moderation and always fresh: processed meats such as ham, bacon and sausages contain nitrates, which are synthetic preservatives that can lead to cell damage if eaten in excess. It's easy to adapt lots of recipes to be meat-free, and I always try to have more than one 'meat-free Monday' in the week! Try my Mushroom and Chestnut Lancashire Hotpot with Sweet Potatoes and Thyme (see page 114) or Mini Chestnut, Apple and Spinach Wellingtons (see page 246) for a vegetarian spin on classic dishes.

I've also tried to swap red meat for lighter meats like chicken and turkey. There are always lots of great lean chicken recipes in my books and this one is no exception (you must cook the Chicken Souvlaki with Kale and Tomato Salad and Tzatziki on page 220). I've also created some great meals containing, of all things, turkey mince, like my very healthy Turkey Meatballs with Spaghetti, Oregano and Fennel (see page 144).

Dairy

I now make my own almond milk, as home-made is much tastier and contains far more nutrients then shop bought. A rich, creamy, home-made almond milk is a great way to get bone-friendly calcium, magnesium, vitamin E and healthy fats. This is not to say that you should refrain from buying it. I can only make this milk when I have enough time to do so; the rest of the time I get it from the shop. I use almond milk instead of regular milk in recipes like my Blueberry and Cinnamon Breakfast Oaty Muffins (see page 26), and it also makes a wonderful base for smoothies or ice cream, like my Hazelnut 'Ella' Chocolate Ice Cream (With a Touch of Coconut) (see page 292).

Instead of butter I use extra virgin olive oil. It's a very healthy fat, containing polyphenols, which have anti-inflammatory and antioxidant properties. New research suggests that they can also trigger powerful anti-ageing and longevity effects in the body.

Vegetables

I am trying to add more green vegetables to my life due to the essential nutrients that come with eating a good amount of raw and/ or lightly cooked veg every day. To make things as easy as possible, I whip up a big batch of my Power Food Greens Salad with Cavolo Nero, Watercress, Spring Onions and Sesame (see page 80) to add to meals throughout the week. I believe that eating lightly cooked and raw food is better for me, as well as being easier and quicker to prepare!

Smoothies and shakes are the best way of giving yourself a power mix of nutrients to help you feel good inside and out. Grab a powerful blender like a NutriBullet to get going. If you want a beauty treatment in a drink, try my Love the Skin You're In (see page 50), or if your digestive system needs a boost, mix up Love In My Tummy (see page 62).

Fresh herbs and spices

The addition of fresh herbs and dry spices can transform a mediocre dish into something really very tasty. And it's not just about the taste benefits, either. When used with carbohydrates, cinnamon has a beneficial effect on the absorption and control of glucose – turning it into a sustained energy releaser. And turmeric is a powerful anti-inflammatory and immune booster. Make sure you use it with black pepper to increase its absorption.

Sugar/sugar substitutes

I use dates a lot throughout this book instead of refined sugar. Dates do contain sugar, but the benefit of using dates as a sweetener above regular refined sugar is that you are getting loads of goodness, like selenium, copper, potassium and magnesium, along with B vitamins and antioxidants – it's a winner! Other bonuses are that they do not produce such a blood-sugar high when you eat them, as the fibre in them slows all that down. Research also now points to the benefits from dates in inflammatory conditions, cancer prevention and metabolic health. People often say to me, 'Well, why can I not use something like honey or maple syrup?' Of course, I use them sometimes too, but they are only marginally better for you than regular refined white sugar, as they are very much still sugars. Dates are not the cheapest things in the world, but they're easily available and are simply delicious, especially the sweetest variety of all, which we can find easily in UK shops,

the Medjool, which has a soft, sweet caramel flavour with honey undertones. Dates can be chopped and added to dishes like my Steamed Sweet Brussels Sprouts with Chestnut, Ginger and Nutmeg (page 252) or made into a Date Purée Paste (see page 46) and, used in place of liquid sweeteners like honey and maple syrup, added to smoothies like my Bright-eyed and Bushy-tailed (see page 60), Cinnamon Protein Pancakes (see page 158) and even savoury dishes like the Baked Chipotle Chilli Haddock with a Red Pepper and Red Onion Relish, with Capers and Parsley (see page 188).

Supplements

With a high-quality diet, nutritional supplements are often not required. Depending on our diets, we may be deficient in some nutrients, but unfortunately this can only be discovered with lengthy blood tests. As we do not have much sun in the UK, vitamin D is one of the nutrients that is so often lacking in our diets. Vitamin D is important for strong bones, a healthy immune system and protecting against many chronic diseases. With very few dietary sources, sunshine is our primary source of this vitamin, and during the winter months many of us become deficient. The recommended dose is 1,000 IU of vitamin D3 per day through the winter months.

Selenium is another nutrient that is very often deficient in many of our diets. Selenium is a trace mineral with many important benefits for immunity, inflammation, thyroid function, and cancer protection. Yet many in Western Europe, including the UK, are deficient due to very low nutrient levels in our soil. The recommended dose in the UK is 100mcg of selenium per day for men and 50mcg of selenium per day for women.

I hope that you will find these recipes easy to prepare and tasty, and the ingredients easy to find. I developed them so they would be family-friendly and as faff-free as possible – and, of course, healthy too!

I always love seeing people giving my recipes a go. Why not take a photo of your creations and post it to me with #EatingWellMadeEasy?

Instagram: instagram.com/lorrainepascale
Twitter: @lorrainepascale
Facebook: facebook.com/lorrainepascale
YouTube: youtube.com/officiallpascale
Website: www.lorrainepascale.com

Happy Eating!!

Lorraine Pascale
xxx

THE START IS WHAT STOPS MOST PEOPLE.

Lazy Sunday mornings

A good start to the day

70k followers!
Thank you so much
for your support!
LP 🤍 xxx

avocado and poached egg on rye with basil and sea salt

spelt flour bread with cranberries,
hazelnuts and thyme

blackberry and blueberry ginger yogurt pots

blueberry and cinnamon breakfast oaty muffins

quick almond, apricot and vanilla muesli

peanut butter and banana muffins

simple porridge with cinnamon, seeds and dates

feta, spinach and basil omelette muffins

slow-cooker baked apples with pecans,
raisins and allspice

breakfast lettuce cups with scrambled eggs,
spring onion and smoked haddock

peanut butter apple slice sandwiches

creamy home-made unsweetened nut milk

date purée paste

smoothies

a good start
to the day

avocado and poached egg on rye with basil and sea salt

serves 2

Not reinventing the wheel, but this really is my absolute favourite breakfast. It is very filling so to make it a little lighter, simply remove the avocado bit of the dish. When eating this, I find the best bites are the ones that have every element on the fork to get the full impact of this tasty dish.

4 free-range eggs

1 tbsp white wine vinegar

4 slices of wholegrain rye bread (that extra dark stuff)

1 perfectly ripe avocado, halved, peeled and de-stoned

Handful of baby spinach (about 50g)

A few fresh basil leaves

Sea salt and freshly ground black pepper

Preheat the grill to high or have your toaster ready on stand-by.

Bring a wide pan of water to a gentle simmer over a low–medium heat and add the vinegar. Crack an egg into a ramekin or small jug and carefully pour it into the water. Repeat with the remaining eggs. Leave to cook gently for 3 minutes.

Meanwhile, toast the bread under the grill or in the toaster until crisp and golden. Once toasted, place two slices on each serving plate and scoop out half an avocado onto the slices on each plate. Spread it out evenly, season with a little salt and pepper and then top with spinach leaves.

Using a slotted spoon, carefully remove the eggs from the water. The whites should be fully cooked but the yolks still quite soft. I like to blot the base of the spoon on kitchen paper so that the eggs are not too 'wet'. Sit an egg on top of each pile of spinach, sprinkle the basil leaves over and serve straight away.

spelt flour bread
with cranberries,
hazelnuts and thyme

makes 1 loaf

I suspect that you, like me, don't have any time to faff around in the morning making loaves of bread, but there is nothing like both the taste and the smell of a freshly baked loaf, straight from the oven. So the way to an easier breakfast loaf life is to make this in advance, slice it up, lay the slices out on a tray or trays that will fit into your freezer and then once frozen, bag the slices up. In the mornings, simply reach into the freezer for a slice of bread, pop into the toaster and toast away to your liking. Top with poached eggs, scrambled eggs or some smoked salmon for a well-balanced breakfast.

100g self-raising flour
200g wholemeal flour
150g spelt flour, plus extra for dusting
2 tsp baking powder
¼ tsp fine salt
1 tbsp extra virgin olive oil
50g dried cranberries or raisins
50g hazelnuts, roughly chopped
1 tbsp chopped fresh thyme

Preheat the oven to 200°C (fan 180°C), 400°F, Gas Mark 6. Place a baking sheet in the oven. This will give the bread extra 'bottom' heat when it cooks and the bread will have a nice base crust and a good rise.

Put the flours, baking powder and salt into a large bowl, stir everything together and make a well in the centre. Pour in 225ml water and the extra virgin olive oil. Mix everything together well with a spoon until it starts to come together and then get your (clean) hands in. Squidge the dough together, gathering up all of those stray bits to give a nice ball.

Place a little bit of flour on your work surface and pop the dough down on it. Flatten it out a bit and then put the cranberries, hazelnuts and thyme on top. Bring in all the edges of the dough to cover the fruit and nuts in the middle, flip the whole thing over and knead it a little to get everything nice and uniform within the dough. Shape the dough into a ball about 15–20cm across (and about 5–8cm deep).

Remove the baking sheet from the oven, sprinkle on some flour and sit the dough on top. Rub some flour on a wooden spoon handle. Hold the handle horizontally just above the dough and push it down onto the ball, all the way through to the bottom until you reach the baking sheet. Then lift the spoon out, giving it a little wiggle to get it out of the dough if need be. Repeat this in the opposite direction to give a cross mark. Sprinkle the bread with a little flour and then bake at the top of the oven for about 35 minutes or until the bread sounds hollow when it is tapped underneath. Once cooked, remove from the oven, leave to cool on a wire rack and then serve.

blackberry and blueberry ginger yogurt pots

serves 4

These berries don't need much cooking time to stew down. However, you can change the fruits to apples, pears or even quinces and cook them in the slow cooker on low for about 5 hours. Let the slow cooker revolution continue! Best way forward for this brekky is to cook the fruit (frozen works well, too) and oats in batches so you have enough to last you throughout the week.

300g blueberries

300g blackberries

2 tsp ground ginger

1cm piece of fresh ginger, peeled and very finely chopped

1 tsp sunflower oil or a little spray oil

100g oats

500g natural yogurt

Put the berries in a wide, medium pan with the ground and fresh ginger and 2 teaspoons of water and place over a low heat. Cook for about 10 minutes, stirring occasionally, until the berries are soft and mushy. Remove from the heat and leave to cool completely before serving.

Meanwhile, using some kitchen paper, rub a medium non-stick frying pan with the oil or spritz with a little spray oil and set it over a medium heat. Add the oats and cook for 4–5 minutes, tossing frequently, until just catching colour. Remove from the heat and leave to cool completely before serving.

Divide the yogurt, berries and oats among four bowls and serve.

blueberry and cinnamon breakfast oaty muffins

makes 16

I have lots of people asking me to create gluten-free recipes that do not just rely on the gluten-free flour that can be found in the shops. I have experimented with almond flour (ground almonds), but find that the resulting bakes can be quite heavy, which does not suit all baked goods, and also highly calorific. So while I use ground almonds in some things, I do like to use oats in others. Oats are often processed in factories where other products containing gluten are used, so be sure to look for actual gluten-free oats on the label if you are avoiding gluten. I found them in my high street chain health food shop and the supermarkets also. The cinnamon in this recipe adds a lovely taste to the blueberries, as well as helping regulate blood sugar levels.

300g gluten-free oats

450ml unsweetened almond milk

125g Medjool dates, pitted

1 free-range egg

2 tsp gluten-free baking powder

2 tsp ground cinnamon

150g fresh blueberries

Preheat the oven to 180°C (fan 160°C), 350°F, Gas Mark 4. Line a muffin tin with 12 paper muffin cases.

Put 275g of the oats into a food processor and blitz them until they form a fine powder. Then add the almond milk, dates, egg, baking powder and cinnamon and blitz together to give a fairly smooth and sloppy mixture.

Tip the mixture into a large bowl and gently stir in the blueberries until well mixed through. Divide the mixture evenly among the 12 muffin cases. I like to use a mechanical ice cream scoop to do this.

Sprinkle over the remaining oats and bake in the oven for 20–25 minutes or until the muffins are cooked through.

Remove from the oven and leave to cool a little before tucking in.

be sure to find gluten-free oats
if you're avoiding gluten

quick almond, apricot and vanilla muesli

makes 925g

Trying to get my daughter to eat breakfast in the morning is no mean feat. In fact I know how hard it is for most people to have breakfast due to factors such as time or just not feeling like eating so early. I do find though that if people can choose what they like in their muesli, the inclination to eat it becomes a little stronger. I have left the oats untoasted here to go with the quick theme, but the oats can be spread over a baking tray and cooked for about 30 minutes at 160°C (fan 140°C), 320°F, Gas Mark 3 to give them a roasty flavour. So many of us have some dried fruit (often raisins) in the cupboard, so do add whichever you have to hand.

400g porridge oats

150g dried apricots, roughly chopped

150g whole almonds

175g mixed seeds (like pumpkin, sunflower, linseeds, poppy and sesame seeds)

Pinch of salt (optional)

50g toasted flaked almonds

Seeds from 1 vanilla pod

Mix all of the ingredients together in a large bowl until evenly combined. Pour into an airtight container.

Serve with regular milk or an unsweetened nut milk (hazelnut or almond are my favourites) of your choice.

peanut butter
and
banana muffins

makes 12

These freeze beautifully. Simply pop the cooled muffins on a tray and into the freezer, then once they are frozen, bag them up. I do it this way so that the muffins do not all stick together during freezing.

300g crunchy peanut butter (use one that only adds salt to the ingredients, never sugar)

200ml unsweetened almond milk

100g oats, plus 2 tbsp extra for the topping

75g spelt flour (wholemeal will work, too)

2 large ripe bananas, peeled and roughly broken into pieces

6 Medjool dates, pitted

1 free-range egg

1 tsp baking powder

½–1 tsp ground cinnamon

Preheat the oven to 180°C (fan 160°C), 350°F, Gas Mark 4. Line a 12-hole muffin tin with muffin cases.

Put all of the ingredients (except the topping oats) in a food processor and blitz for about 30 seconds until well combined, to give a fairly smooth paste.

Divide the mixture evenly among the 12 muffin cases and sprinkle over the extra oats.

Bake in the oven for 30 minutes or until a skewer inserted into the centre of one of the muffins comes out clean.

Once cooked, remove from the oven and leave to cool a little before enjoying.

simple porridge with cinnamon, seeds and dates

serves 4-6

I am in the habit of making porridge in the morning with a few blueberries and a pinch of cinnamon if I have the time, but cooking something that has more flavour makes breakfast a lot more interesting and tasty and, with the addition of protein-rich seeds, nutritious.

200g porridge oats (not quick cook)

1 litre water, home-made nut milk or semi-skimmed milk

3 Medjool dates, pitted and roughly chopped

Seeds from ½ vanilla pod

¼ tsp ground cinnamon

Good grating of nutmeg

1 pear, peeled, cored and finely chopped

Pinch of salt

Handful of mixed seeds or nuts

Place the oats in a medium pan with the water or milk (or a mixture of both), dates, vanilla seeds, cinnamon and nutmeg. Cook over a low–medium heat for about 10–15 minutes, stirring regularly, until the oats are nice and soft and creamy. Stir the pear in halfway through cooking and add the salt.

Sprinkle over the nuts or seeds and serve at once.

feta, spinach
and basil
omelette muffins

makes 8

I like to make things in my cupcake tray that are not cupcakes. Often. And these quasi-muffin/omelettes are one of my favourites. A good thing to do is to make a whole load and store them in the fridge for lunches, brunches and snacks for the family to enjoy without having to make them fresh each time. They will keep for a couple of days in the fridge.

muffins

Spray oil or sunflower oil, for greasing

8 free-range eggs

8 sun-dried tomatoes, drained well and roughly chopped

Large handful of baby leaf spinach (about 25g), roughly chopped

Good pinch of freshly grated nutmeg

125g feta cheese, roughly broken into bite-sized pieces

Few fresh basil leaves

Sea salt and freshly ground black pepper

salad

100g rocket, watercress or mixed salad leaves

3 tbsp extra virgin olive oil

1 tbsp balsamic vinegar

Sea salt and freshly ground black pepper

Preheat the oven to 170°C (fan 150°C), 325°F, Gas Mark 3. Grease 8 holes of a muffin tin with the spray or sunflower oil and set aside.

Put the eggs, tomato, spinach, nutmeg and salt (just a little bit as the feta is very salty) and pepper into a large jug and whisk together until combined. Divide the mixture evenly among the 8 muffin holes and then sprinkle over the feta cheese.

Bake in the oven for about 20 minutes or until the muffins have risen slightly, are firm to the touch and lightly golden. Then, remove from the oven and leave to cool a little.

Place the salad leaves on a large serving plate. Whisk the oil and vinegar together in a small bowl or mug with a little salt and pepper and pour over the leaves.

Using a small, sharp knife, loosen the edges of each muffin from the tin and carefully pop them out. Arrange them on top of the salad leaves. Rip up the basil leaves, scatter them over the top and serve.

enjoy these soft delights with
their crunchy topping cold or
warm: they're perfect either way

slow-cooker baked apples with pecans, raisins and allspice

serves 6

The ideal would be to pop these in the slow cooker at night and then wake up and have them ready and soft for the morning. I did try this but alas, and of course, in the morning the apples were a soggy (but tasty) heap of goo in the centre with crispy bits of breakfastness clinging defiantly to the sides of my slow cooker. Needless to say, I popped my spoon in the goo and ate as much as I could. These apples do not need overnight to cook so the overnight dream does not work. However, I have cooked these ahead of time and then just eaten them cold in the morning. If you are not against using microwaves and want yours hot then of course you could zap the cold apples in there for a couple of minutes.

50g porridge oats

Pinch of salt

25g raisins or cranberries

1 tsp ground cinnamon

½ tsp ground ginger

½ tsp allspice

6 Granny Smith apples
(Braeburn would work well, too)

to serve

Handful of chopped pecans

Natural yogurt

Mix together the porridge oats, salt, raisins or cranberries, cinnamon, ginger and allspice in a small bowl.

Cut about 1–2cm off the tops of the apples and set aside. Then, using an apple corer, remove the core of each apple. Sit the apple bases in the bowl of your slow cooker.

Using a teaspoon, divide the mixture among the apples in the slow cooker. I like to use the handle of the spoon to pack the mixture into the core cavity and then spoon the excess onto their flat tops. Pop the lids back on each one and cover with the slow cooker lid.

Cook in the slow cooker for about 3–4 hours on low. You want the apples to be soft but not so soft that they collapse.

Once cooked, remove from the slow cooker and serve with a handful of chopped pecans and some natural yogurt. These apples are also quite tasty cold from the fridge.

breakfast lettuce cups with scrambled eggs, spring onion and smoked haddock

serves 4

Salmon is lovely but expensive, so I have used haddock here. However, they are as tasty as each other, with salmon coming in more nutritious due to its high content of omega 3. I love to have protein for breakfast as then I stay full until at least midday!

4 iceberg lettuce leaves,
hard ends trimmed

150g smoked haddock or
125g smoked salmon

Knob of butter

10 medium free-range eggs

2 spring onions, trimmed and finely chopped

½ red chilli, deseeded for less heat if
preferred, finely chopped (optional)

Sea salt and freshly ground black pepper

Place the lettuce leaves on a large serving plate and then set aside.

If you are using smoked salmon there is obviously no cooking involved. If using haddock, place it in a microwaveable dish with 1 tablespoon of water. Cover and microwave for about 3 minutes or until the haddock flakes easily. Alternatively, place the fish in a small pan and add 4 tablespoons of water. Cover with a lid and bring the water up to the boil, then reduce the heat and leave to simmer for about 3–4 minutes or until the fish is cooked, flakes easily and is piping hot. Discard the skin and any bones.

Next, place the butter in a medium pan over a low–medium heat. Crack the eggs into a medium jug, season well and beat them together. Once the butter is sizzling, add the eggs and while stirring all the time, cook them for a few minutes until they are softly scrambled, still with a moist and creamy consistency.

Remove from the heat and divide among the four lettuce cups. Arrange the smoked haddock or salmon on top. Sprinkle over the spring onion and chilli, if using, and serve immediately.

peanut butter
apple slice
sandwiches
makes 6

I struggle to have peanut butter in the house without consuming the entire jar very quickly. These little bites not only make a quick breakfast, but also a tasty anytime snack.

2 large Granny Smith apples

6 tbsp peanut butter

25g raisins, dried cranberries or goji berries (optional)

Remove the apple cores using an apple corer. Cut each apple into six even-sized slices (about 1cm thick) across their midriff (as opposed to from base to top).

Lay the apple slices out in pairs so that each apple 'round' has a mate, which is more or less the same size as them. Put the bases in one row and the tops in the row above them.

Spread each base with 1 tablespoon of peanut butter and sprinkle over the dried fruit, if using. Pop the tops on each one and serve straight away.

creamy home-made
unsweetened nut milk

makes 450ml

A rich, creamy, home-made almond milk is a great way to get bone-friendly calcium, magnesium, vitamin E and healthy fats. This recipe uses almonds, but experiment with different nuts, such as cashews or hazelnuts. Pumpkin seed milk sounds bonkers, but it is actually really nice, so do give this a try, too! The nuts require an overnight soak, but aside from that, the milk is quite simple and quick to make.

165g blanched almonds

Seeds of 1 vanilla pod (optional)

1 Medjool date, pitted (optional)

Put the almonds in a bowl and pour over enough water to cover the almonds by about 2cm. Leave the almonds to soak for about 8 hours or overnight, then pour off this soaking water and rinse them gently under cold water. Pop the almonds in a blender and add 450ml water. Blend the almonds for about 4–5 minutes, scraping down the sides two or three times to make sure everything is blended in nicely.

There are all sorts of fancy bags and whatnot to do the next bit in, but I just like to use a piece of muslin/cheesecloth. Put a large sieve over a bowl and line the sieve with it so that the fabric overlaps the side a lot. Then tip the almond mushy mixture into the sieve. I like to get my hands in and really squidge all the liquid (almond milk) from the almonds. Once you have got as much liquid as possible out of the mixture, put the strainer and the almond mush aside and taste the almond milk.

Add some vanilla seeds and a date, if using, and mix together well. Keep in the fridge for up to 2 days.

date
purée
paste
makes 300g

Use this paste in dressings, on cereals and in some savoury dishes where honey or maple syrup is specified to sweeten.

200g of Medjool dates, pitted

Seeds of ½ a vanilla pod

Place the dates in a bowl and cover with water. Leave to soak for 1 hour. After 1 hour, drain the dates, but reserve the soaking liquid. Place the dates in a blender or Nutribullet and then add the vanilla seeds and about 3 tablespoons of the soaking liquid. Blitz together well to form a paste, which should be the consistency of thick Greek yogurt. Add a little more water if yours is a bit too thick. Discard the rest of the soaking water, then scrape the date paste into a container and keep in the fridge for up to about a week.

dates contain lots of fibre, so they do not produce
such a blood sugar high when you eat them

smoothies

What better way to start the day than a glass of pure goodness? The smoothies I've come up with and love aren't just going to pump you full of fruit sugars like some do – especially those 'healthy' blends you find in chiller cabinets – they're chock-full of vegetables and other nutrient-rich foods to keep you going till lunch and give your brain, skin and tum a boost too.

breakfast green
super smoothie
with kale and pear

p.56

spring
clean
detox

p.52

love
the skin
you're in

p.50

instant
karma
p.58

bright eyed
and
bushy tailed
p.60

love
in my
tummy
p.62

energising bunny
p.54

love the skin you're in

makes 350ml

There is so much focus in the beauty world on treating the skin from the outside and not so much about treating your skin from the inside. I have learned that what we eat has a massive impact on how our skin looks. This drink has a power mix of nutrients in it that help to hydrate, strengthen and smooth the skin, along with offering anti-ageing properties and helping to minimise skin damage from the sun. This is a good one for kiddies due to its chocolate and strawberry combination and you are sneaking other veggies into it, too!

25g dark chocolate (85% cocoa solids), roughly chopped or 1 tbsp unsweetened cocoa powder

150ml unsweetened almond or rice milk or water, at room temperature

100g strawberries, hulled

½ ripe tomato, roughly chopped

½ carrot, peeled and roughly chopped

3 walnut halves

¼ tsp ground cinnamon

Melt the chocolate in a small pan on the hob or in a bowl in the microwave. Remove and leave to cool to room temperature. Skip this step if using cocoa powder instead.

Put all the ingredients in a blender or NutriBullet and blitz for 30 seconds until smooth. Pour into a glass and serve.

blackcurrants can be substituted for blueberries or strawberries in this 'spring clean' wonder drink

spring
clean
detox

makes about 375ml

This is the drink I like to have when I feel I need a bit of an internal spring clean. Like some other healthy smoothies and shakes, this is not the sexiest tasting or looking drink in the world, but the benefits are huge. So sometimes after a big night out (not that they come very often) or when I am feeling a little under the weather, out comes that kale and matcha! Matcha green tea is something that I buy on the internet and also in some supermarkets. It is quite pricey, so if you cannot find it, then just leave it out altogether. Blackcurrants can be substituted with blueberries or strawberries as they can be tricky to find. I love putting blackcurrants in my smoothies and shakes so I buy a massive 3kg bag of frozen ones online (at a really good price!) and then store them in the freezer for when I need them. The green tea in this has a little caffeine in it, which means I would not give this drink to the kiddies.

30g kale, woody stalks removed

50g fresh or frozen blackcurrants

1 small apple, cored and roughly chopped

Leaves and stalks of 3 fresh
flat-leaf parsley stems

Juice of ½ lemon or lime (to stabilise the
green tea compounds)

½ tsp matcha green tea

1 Medjool date, pitted (optional)

Place everything into a NutriBullet or blender with 225ml water and blitz for 30 seconds until smooth. Taste and blitz the date in if you prefer it to be a little sweeter. Pour into a glass and serve.

energising
bunny

makes 100ml

Some energy drinks laden with vitamins and minerals will only give you that much-needed boost if you are deficient in the nutrients that they are offering. Unfortunately, the main boost comes from the sugar in the drink. Coffee often gets a bad rap, but in the right amounts has a beneficial role in issues like liver health and helping reduce your risk of getting diabetes and Alzheimer's. Who would have thought it! Long live coffee!

25ml unsweetened almond or rice milk

25g dark chocolate (85% cocoa solids), roughly chopped, or 1 tbsp unsweetened cocoa powder

50ml hot espresso coffee (a double)

1–2 thin slices of red chilli, deseeded for less heat if preferred, or a pinch of chilli flakes

1 tbsp date purée paste (I find I need to use an extra bit if using cocoa powder rather than the chocolate) (see page 46)

Place the milk and chocolate (or cocoa if using) in a small pan over a low heat or in a bowl in the microwave and warm through gently, stirring regularly, until the chocolate has melted.

Pour into a blender or NutriBullet and add the remaining ingredients. Blitz for 30 seconds until smooth. Pour into glasses and serve warm.

top tips

If you prefer a cold drink, simply allow the coffee to cool and then add to the blender with the remaining ingredients. It's advisable to use cocoa powder rather than chocolate here, as the chocolate tends to not blend down very well and gives a grainy texture to the drink.

You can also add 25g mixed berries to the blender or NutriBullet along with the other ingredients for a fruity twist.

breakfast green super smoothie with kale and pear

makes 900ml

I make this sporadically for my breakfast and while I admit this is not chocolate cake, I have grown to rather like the taste. Most of all I like this smoothie for its anti-inflammatory and immune-boosting properties.

125g kale, woody stems removed

2 small pears, cored and roughly chopped (unpeeled)

1 Medjool date, pitted

1cm piece of fresh ginger, peeled

2 tbsp flaxseeds (linseeds)

1 tsp turmeric powder (optional)

Throw everything into a powerful blender with 375ml water and blitz until smooth. You may need to add the kale in batches if it doesn't all fit at once. If you want an ice-cold drink, then add some ice also. Divide into glasses and serve.

instant karma

makes 350ml

I am often doing too much. And if I am not doing too much, I am thinking too much.
I feel it is a modern-day problem – there always seems to be something going on. Instant
karma is a great shake made with tart cherry juice, which helps increase those relaxing,
feel-good chemicals in the body and may help promote better sleep. Ommmmmmm.
I really try only to put recipes in my books where you can get the ingredients from regular
shops, but I bought this cherry juice on the internet as I simply could not find it at any of
the supermarkets, only online and in health food shops. However, I wanted to put it in the
book as it really does help with sleep, which is a problem I experience a lot.

2 ripe kiwis

**50ml tart unsweetened Montmorency
cherry juice (not concentrated) or regular
unsweetened cherry juice**

1 tbsp pumpkin seeds

Wash the kiwis if leaving the skin on or remove and
discard if preferred. Roughly chop the kiwis and pop
them in a NutriBullet or blender along with the cherry
juice, pumpkin seeds and 100ml water.

Blitz for 30 seconds until smooth. Pour into a glass
and serve.

bright-eyed
and
bushy-tailed

makes about 350ml

How many hours a day are you on a computer or phone screen? I know I use the computer way too much. I am not here to say what we should or should not be doing, but hopefully giving simple and easy ways to help us towards a healthier way of eating. It is not much of a looker, but this smoothie has a mix of nutrients that helps promote optimal health of the eyes.

200ml unsweetened almond milk or water

50g fresh or frozen blackcurrants

25g oats

15g spinach

¼ yellow pepper, deseeded and roughly chopped

1 tbsp sunflower seeds

1 tbsp date purée paste (see page 46)

Pop everything into a blender or NutriBullet and blitz for 30 seconds until smooth. Pour into a glass and serve.

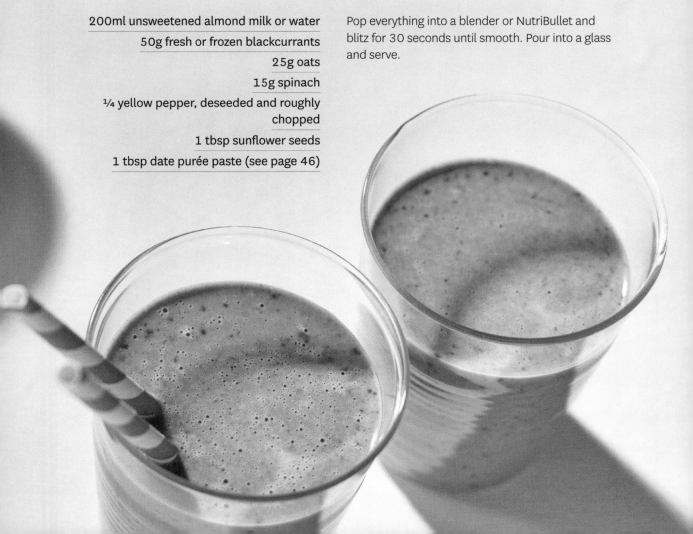

love
in my
tummy
makes 300ml

Cabbage, pineapple, ginger and mint may not be the things you'd think of putting together in a shake, but this unusual mix of ingredients will nourish and relax the tummy and give a boost to your digestive system.

2 large green cabbage leaves (preferably not the tough, outside ones), washed, hard core removed and leaves roughly chopped

75g fresh pineapple (from about 1 thick peeled, decored and diced slice)

2cm piece of fresh ginger, peeled and roughly chopped

⅛ tsp turmeric powder

10 fresh mint leaves

Place everything into a Nutribullet or blender with 100ml filtered water and blitz for 30 seconds until smooth. Pour into a glass and serve.

soothing sag aloo soup

roast red pepper, tomato and caramelised onion
soup with buckwheat

immune-boosting super soup

Vietnamese prawn noodle soup with star anise and cinnamon

lemon, thyme and pepper-crusted chicken
with wholegrain rice

smoked salmon quiche with kale and basil,
and a sesame seed crust

power food greens salad with cavolo nero, watercress,
spring onions and sesame

posh beans on super-quick garlic and thyme bread

quinoa with raisins, walnuts and parsley

steamed chicken salad with cavolo nero, goat's cheese
and pumpkin seeds

sweet potato, kale and leek bubble and squeak with sage

kuku sabzi (spicy herbed frittata)

paprika and cumin-spiced prawn lunch box rice salad

Sichuan bang bang chicken with spicy peanut sauce

goat's cheese and courgette salad with toasted pine nuts

sesame-crusted tuna steaks with quinoa and mango salad
and a ginger soy dressing

light lunches

soothing
sag aloo
soup

serves 4-6

I had this when I was out and about attending meetings the other day and absolutely loved it. This is not a traditional recipe and it is unusual to have this dish in the form of a soup, but I feel it really does work. If you want to make this in its regular form as a vegetable side dish and not as a soup, then just put enough stock into the dish for the potatoes to cook in and soak up all of the liquid.

1 tbsp olive oil

½ tsp mustard seeds

1 tsp ground cumin

1 tsp ground coriander

1 tsp turmeric powder

1 large onion, very finely chopped

2cm piece of fresh ginger, peeled and very finely chopped

2 garlic cloves, very finely chopped

1 red chilli, deseeded for less heat if preferred, very finely chopped

1 litre of a good liquid vegetable stock

1 large waxy potato (about 450g), peeled and cut into 1cm dice

2 tomatoes, roughly diced

125g spinach leaves

½ tin of chickpeas, drained (optional)

Sea salt and freshly ground black pepper

Put the oil in a large pan over a low–medium heat. Add the mustard seeds, cumin, coriander and turmeric and cook for a couple of minutes or until you start to smell the aromas of the spices. Add the onion and ginger and cook for about 10 minutes, stirring regularly until softened. Add the garlic and chilli and cook for 1 minute more.

Gradually pour in the stock, scraping any sticky bits from the bottom of the pan as you go. Stir in the potato and tomato. Bring to the boil and then reduce to simmer for about 15 minutes or until the potatoes are tender. Stir in the spinach, fistfuls at a time, until wilted. Add the chickpeas to heat them through, if using, then season the soup to taste and remove from the heat.

Ladle into bowls and serve.

a warming, fragrant and satisfying lunch – not a soggy sandwich in sight!

roast red pepper, tomato and caramelised onion soup with buckwheat

serves 4-6

I wanted to make as many recipes in this book as faff-free as possible, recognising all too well the need for speed when it comes to mealtimes. But some things cannot be rushed, like making peppers taste as sweet as they can. The only way to do this is by roasting the peppers slowly in a nice hot oven until their skins go wrinkly and blistered and the sugars in the vegetable's flesh have a chance to caramelise. Experiment with chipotle chilli flakes, too, if you can find them, as they add a lovely smokiness to the soup. This is also a great way of getting vitamin C, as half a small red pepper will give each person enough vitamin C for the day! Brilliant.

6 red peppers, halved and deseeded

1 large red onion, quartered

4 garlic cloves, unpeeled

Leaves from 2 sprigs of fresh rosemary

2 tbsp extra virgin olive oil

5 large, ripe tomatoes, halved

1–2 tsp chilli flakes or chipotle chilli flakes, depending how hot you like it (optional)

500ml vegetable or chicken stock

100g buckwheat

Sea salt and freshly ground black pepper

to serve

1 tbsp roughly chopped fresh chives, flat-leaf parsley or coriander

Arrange the peppers (cut-side up) and red onion wedges in a single layer on a large baking tray. Slam the garlic cloves with the side of a large knife to squish them and scatter them over along with the rosemary and salt and pepper to season. Drizzle over the oil and roast in the oven for 20 minutes.

Add the tomato halves, sprinkle over the chilli flakes, if using, and return to the oven to cook for 25 minutes until everything is nicely charred and softened.

Remove from the oven, place the peppers in a medium bowl, cover with cling film and set aside for about 10 minutes. This allows the steam to loosen the skins from the peppers, making them easier to peel.

Returning to the rest of the ingredients on the tray, squeeze the garlic cloves from their skins into a blender. Add the remaining ingredients on the tray, including any juices and sticky bits and set aside.

Once the peppers have had their time, peel the skins off the peppers and add the flesh to the blender. Add half of the stock and blitz until smooth, then add the remaining stock and blitz again.

Pour the soup into a pan and season with salt and pepper if necessary. You can simply warm the soup through and serve at this stage, but I love the addition of the buckwheat. Add the buckwheat, bring to the boil and then turn the heat right down to simmer for about 15 minutes or until the buckwheat is tender.

Divide the soup among serving bowls and serve with a sprinkling of chives, parsley or coriander to finish off this dish nicely.

immune-boosting super soup

serves 4-6

Not a drink, but a soup that will help to boost your immune system. It has been said that there is no food or supplement that can rival mushrooms for their direct immune-boosting benefits. This soup has such a warm, soul-heartening feel to it too: good for the cold winter days, especially when everyone at school/work is sneezing all around you! The turmeric (along with black pepper, which helps its absorption) is something I am starting to use much more often as it is another immune booster and acts as an anti-inflammatory agent (perfect for my knees, which play up a lot!). Add some lemongrass for extra flavour if you like.

1 tbsp sunflower oil

1 onion, finely sliced

400g Jerusalem artichokes, peeled and finely diced

3-4 garlic cloves, crushed

1cm piece of fresh ginger, peeled and finely grated

1.1 litres vegetable stock

100g shitake mushrooms, sliced

100g oyster mushrooms, sliced

1 red chilli, thinly sliced into rings (optional)

1½ tsp turmeric powder

Juice of ½ lime

Leaves from ½ bunch of fresh coriander

Sea salt and a good amount of freshly ground black pepper

Heat the oil in a large pan over a low–medium heat and sauté the onion and Jerusalem artichokes for 8–10 minutes, stirring occasionally, until beginning to soften and turn golden.

Add the garlic and ginger and continue to cook for another minute. Add the stock, mushrooms, chilli, if using, and turmeric, bring to the boil and then reduce the heat to a simmer for about 12–15 minutes until the Jerusalem artichokes are completely tender.

Stir in the lime juice and season to taste with salt and pepper.

Either leave the soup as it is or blend until smooth in a liquidiser or with a stick blender. Finish by stirring the coriander leaves through and serve.

Vietnamese
prawn noodle soup
with star anise
and cinnamon

serves 4

The traditional way to make this soup taste the best is to make your own stock for it; but this soup will taste delightful even if you use a good shop-bought liquid stock. I had this soup in Hanoi, where it is traditionally called pho, pronounced 'fuh', and made with beef or chicken. My version has prawns in for a little variation.

1.5 litres of good chicken, beef, veg or fish stock

3 garlic cloves, very finely chopped

2 red chillies, deseeded for less heat if preferred, very finely chopped

2 sticks of lemon grass, first two layers removed, the white bit finely chopped

3cm piece of fresh ginger, peeled and very finely chopped

3 tbsp soy sauce

10 black peppercorns

3 whole cloves

2 star anise

1 small cinnamon stick

300g rice noodles

400g raw, peeled king prawns

Juice of 1 small lime

1–4 tsp fish sauce (optional)

to serve

Sriracha and/or hoisin sauce

Small handful of fresh Thai basil leaves (optional)

Put the stock in a large pan with the garlic, chillies (reserving a small handful for garnishing later if liked), lemon grass, ginger, soy sauce, peppercorns, cloves, star anise and cinnamon, bring to the boil and then reduce the heat to simmer for 10 minutes.

Add the noodles and continue to simmer for as long as the packet says they need to cook. Add the prawns 3–4 minutes before the end of the noodle cooking time. The noodles should be tender and the prawns turned pink and cooked through.

Remove the peppercorns, whole cloves, star anise and cinnamon stick if you like (and if you can fish them out!). Add the lime juice and then taste the soup. Add more soy sauce or some fish sauce if you think it needs it, tasting as you go. Divide among four serving bowls and serve immediately with the any reserved chilli and some Thai basil leaves, if using, scattered over on top.

lemon, thyme
and pepper-crusted
chicken with
wholegrain rice

serves 2

An easy-peasy dish for a quick lunch or supper that hardly needs a recipe. The way to make this work best is to use oodles of black pepper, giving the surface of the chicken an almost crust-like appearance.

200g wholegrain rice

Finely grated zest and juice of 1 lemon

2 tbsp freshly ground black pepper

2 tsp fine sea salt

Leaves from 4 sprigs of fresh thyme

2 skinless, boneless chicken breasts

2 tsp olive oil or butter

to serve

1 tbsp roughly chopped fresh flat-leaf parsley (optional)

Put the rice on to cook according to the packet instructions, adding the lemon zest along with the water; reserving the juice.

Toss the pepper, salt and thyme leaves together and set aside.

Place the chicken breasts, spaced apart, on a large sheet of parchment paper and top with another sheet of paper. Bash them out evenly using a rolling pin or meat mallet until about 1.5cm thick. Press the chicken into the pepper mix to evenly coat both sides.

Heat the oil in a large frying pan over a medium–high heat. Cook the chicken for about 3 minutes on each side until golden, crusty and cooked through, but still lovely and moist. Remove from the heat and slice each breast into 1cm thick strips.

Once the rice is cooked, drain if necessary and then divide it between the serving plates. Arrange the chicken strips on top, drizzle over the lemon juice, sprinkle with parsley, if liked, and serve. Some greens or a salad go with this one nicely.

don't be shy with the black pepper, and be sure to grind it fresh – it's worlds away from the ready-ground stuff

smoked salmon quiche with kale and basil, and a sesame seed crust

serves 4

I have written many quiche recipes and usually they are mushroom with a little ham, but smoked salmon in a quiche gives a lot of flavour and works beautifully with the basil. The spelt pastry is so easy to make, but if you can find a good wholemeal ready-made version in the shops, then do use that instead. Hot smoked trout can replace the smoked salmon for some variation and broccoli could easily replace the kale. Smoked salmon is not an everyday treat, but when my wallet allows, I do try to buy the MSC-certified wild salmon over farmed as it is said to be better for you. Having said that, it is not as cheap and it is about making small changes here and there where it is possible, so regular smoked salmon will also be okay. With this dish I often serve the Tomato, Onion and Caper Salad with Anchovies and Basil (but without the anchovies as the smoked salmon is enough) found on page 206. >

smoked salmon quiche
with kale and basil
and a sesame seed crust
cont.

sesame seed crust

3 tbsp sesame seeds

225g wholemeal spelt flour, plus extra for dusting

75g unsalted butter

1 egg

Olive oil or butter, for greasing

Preheat the oven to 180°C (fan 160°C), 350°F, Gas Mark 4.

Toast the sesame seeds in a small dry frying pan over a medium heat until fragrant and golden. Tip onto a plate and leave to cool.

Meanwhile, grease a 20cm straight-sided, loose-bottomed flan or cake tin (2.5cm deep) and set it on a baking tray.

Once the sesame seeds are cool, tip them and the remaining pastry ingredients, along with 3 tablespoons of water, into a food processor. Whiz together until they form damp crumbs.

Alternatively, to make by hand, put the flour and butter into a large bowl. Pick up bits of the mixture with the tips of your fingers and rub your thumb into your fingers to blend the ingredients together, allowing it to fall back into the bowl. Keep doing this until the mixture resembles fine breadcrumbs. Stir the sesame seeds through. Lightly beat the egg in a small bowl and stir into the crumbs really well with a small knife until it starts to form lumps. Add 3 tablespoons of water to bring it together.

filling

1 tbsp olive oil or butter

1 large onion, finely sliced

125g crème fraîche
(use low-fat if you fancy it)

125g natural yogurt
(use low-fat if you fancy it)

5 free-range eggs

60g kale, woody stems removed
and leaves finely sliced

100g smoked salmon slices (preferably wild
and MSC-certified), torn into bite-sized pieces

Sea salt and freshly ground black pepper

to serve

Leaves from ½ bunch of fresh basil

*serve with a simple
lightly dressed
green salad*

Dust a clean work surface with a little flour and tip the dough out onto it. Bring it together into a smooth ball then roll it out to the thickness of two-thirds of that of a pound coin (about 2mm) to give a roughly 22cm circle (slightly larger than the diameter of the tin).

Carefully lower the pastry into the prepared tin, easing it against the bottom and edges. Use a small, sharp knife to trim the excess pastry off the top rim, using bits of the excess to seal up holes or cracks if necessary. Scrunch up a circular piece of baking parchment a little larger than the tin, then unscrunch and sit it in the pastry case. Tip in ceramic baking beans or dried beans and bake for 20 minutes.

Meanwhile, make the filling. Heat the oil or butter in a medium pan over a low–medium heat. Add the onion and cook down for about 10 minutes or until soft, stirring occasionally. Meanwhile, beat the crème fraîche, yogurt and eggs together in a large bowl until combined. Stir in the kale, season and set aside.

After the pastry has been cooking for 20 minutes, remove the paper and beans and return the pastry case to the oven for a further 5 minutes or until the pastry is cooked, the base is sandy to the touch and it looks lightly golden brown.

Once softened, remove the onion from the heat and leave to cool. Once cool, stir into the kale mix.

Once the pastry case is cooked, remove from the oven and pour in the kale mixture. Arrange the smoked salmon on top. Bake for 35 minutes, or until the salmon is catching colour and the quiche cooked through to the centre. Remove and allow to cool a little. Carefully remove from the tin, cut into quarters and top with freshly torn basil.

power food greens salad with cavolo nero, watercress, spring onions and sesame

serves 4-6

There are days when I like preparing meals and days when I feel less like it. And if there is one thing I often forget to cook, which I really should, it is green veg. I am trying to reverse that habit, knowing full well the essential nutrients that come with eating a good amount of raw and/or lightly cooked veg every day. To make things easier for myself and any other members of the family who may want to eat it, I make a big container full of this and keep it in the fridge, ready to serve alongside things such as chicken, fish or steak. It keeps in the fridge for about 3 days.

3 tsp sesame oil

Juice of ¼ lemon

150g cavolo nero, woody stems removed, cut into thin strips

110g watercress

3 spring onions, finely chopped

100g pak choi, trimmed and cut into thin strips

2 tsp sesame seeds

Pomegranate seeds (optional)

Put the sesame oil into a medium bowl with the lemon juice and add the cavolo nero. Mix this all together and then get your hands in and massage the cavolo nero leaves a little. This helps the leaves to tenderise.

Add the watercress, spring onions, pak choi and sesame seeds and stir everything together so it is all combined. Sprinkle the pomegranate seeds on top, if using, and then serve.

posh beans on super-quick garlic and thyme bread

serves 4

This is not something that you can just grab from the cupboard and whip up in moments. It needs a little preparation beforehand for a heart-warming and comforting, filling lunch. I am making my own bread in this recipe, which is full of flavour and refined sugar free, but for a shortcut, just buy a loaf and make the topping in super-quick time. It is a little bit naughty (though everything in moderation), but adding some crispy bacon or ham (preferably nitrate-free) would be divine. A drizzle of extra virgin olive oil to finish will help the body to absorb the nutrients in the tomato sauce.

bread

425g spelt flour, plus extra for dusting

5 spring onions, finely chopped

3–4 garlic cloves, depending how garlicky you like it, very finely chopped

1 tbsp baking powder

1 tbsp finely grated Parmesan cheese (optional)

Leaves from 1 large handful of fresh thyme (about 2 tbsp)

1 large pinch of dried chilli flakes or chilli powder

1 tsp fine sea salt

Preheat the oven to 200°C (fan 180°C), 400°F, Gas Mark 6.

First, to make the bread, simply put all of the ingredients in a large bowl, add 225ml of warm water (from the tap) and mix together well. If the dough is feeling a bit dry, then add a tablespoon more warm water to bring it all together.

Lightly dust your work surface with flour and knead the dough for a moment or two to give a big ball, about 13cm wide and 4cm thick, with a nice taut top. I tuck the edges of the dough underneath the ball, which makes the top nice and tight, resulting in a much prettier loaf coming out of the oven. Sprinkle a baking sheet with a little flour, pop the dough on to it and then use a sharp knife to make three to five >

posh beans on
super-quick garlic
and thyme bread
cont.

beans

1 tbsp olive oil

1 onion, finely chopped

2 garlic cloves, finely chopped

2 x 400g tins of chopped tomatoes

1 tsp Dijon or English mustard

2 tbsp tomato purée

Leaves from 1 handful of fresh thyme
(about 1 tbsp)

2 x 400g tins of cannellini beans or
chickpeas, drained

Sea salt and freshly ground black pepper

to serve

Handful of fresh flat-leaf parsley leaves,
finely chopped

Extra virgin olive oil (optional)

slashes on top. Bake in the oven for 30–35 minutes or until the loaf is firm to the touch and sounding hollow when tapped underneath.

As the bread bakes, make your beans mixture. Heat the oil in a medium sauté pan over a medium heat. Fry the onion for 5–6 minutes, stirring from time to time, until it just starts to go golden brown. I like to have a bit of bite to my onions in this dish. Then add the garlic and cook for 1 minute more. Tip in the tomatoes, mustard, tomato purée, thyme and a little salt and pepper, mix this all together and bring to the boil. Reduce the heat to simmer for about 20 minutes until the mixture is reduced and thickened, stirring it from time to time so that it does not catch on the bottom. Then add the beans or chickpeas and cook for a further 5 minutes to warm through. Adjust seasoning if necessary.

Once the bread is cooked, remove it from the oven and let it cool down for a few minutes. Then, holding one side with an oven glove, trim the opposite ends (the cook's treat!) and cut the loaf into eight even-sized slices. Toast the slices of bread in your toaster or under a hot grill until golden.

Arrange two slices of toast on each serving plate, matching any smaller ones with larger ones to even them out. Spoon piles of the bean mix on top, sprinkle with parsley, drizzle with extra virgin olive oil, if using, and serve.

quinoa with raisins, walnuts and parsley

serves 4–6

I am a great lover of batch-making stuff and this is one for lunches and dinners that lasts for 2–3 days in the fridge. Replace the raisins with dates, apricots or even figs, change up the parsley by using coriander and finish off the dish with pomegranate seeds for a jewelled look. This is the perfect accompaniment for the Chermoula Roast Salmon on page 266.

250g quinoa

50g walnuts or pine nuts, roughly chopped

75g raisins

Juice of 1 lemon

1 tbsp extra virgin olive oil

Leaves from ½ bunch of fresh flat-leaf parsley, really finely chopped

Sea salt and freshly ground black pepper

Put the quinoa on to cook according to the packet instructions.

As the quinoa cooks, put the walnuts or pine nuts in a small frying pan with no oil over a medium heat and toast the nuts for 3–4 minutes or until golden brown. Remove from the pan, tip into a large bowl and set aside.

Once the quinoa is cooked, drain it really well and tip it in on top of the nuts. Add the raisins, lemon juice, oil and parsley and mix everything together well. Add enough salt and pepper to taste and serve.

steamed chicken salad with cavolo nero, goat's cheese and pumpkin seeds

serves 4-6

I once did a job in Atlanta, had a couple of hours to spare and headed for a restaurant just outside the mall. It was a healthy eating restaurant, but with dishes so delectable you really could not tell they were healthy. I sat by the kitchen as I like to do and watched a young chef artfully tearing the stems from the cavolo nero, which prompted me to order the cavolo nero salad. The leaves were tender and soft as they had been massaged with extra virgin olive oil, which tenderises the leaves and helps us to absorb more of the fat-soluble nutrients from cavolo nero's rich source of goodness.

chicken

4 skinless, boneless chicken breasts

Juice of 1 lemon

3cm piece of fresh ginger, peeled and very finely chopped

1 garlic clove, very finely chopped

Leaves from 4 sprigs of fresh thyme

½ tsp turmeric powder

Sea salt and freshly ground black pepper

To cook the chicken, put a steamer pan with a little water in the bottom over a high heat. Alternatively, preheat the oven to 200°C (fan 180°C), 400°F, Gas Mark 6.

Arrange the chicken breasts in a single layer on a large square of tin foil. Mix the lemon juice, ginger, garlic, thyme and turmeric together with salt and pepper, then pour this over the chicken, tossing the breasts to coat. Scrunch the foil up over the chicken to create a sealed parcel and place it either into the steamer, popping the lid on to cover, or onto a baking tray and into the oven. Either way, cook the chicken for about 20 minutes or until cooked through. >

steamed chicken salad
with cavolo nero,
goat's cheese and
pumpkin seeds
cont.

salad

400g cavolo nero, woody stems removed and
very finely sliced

2 tsp extra virgin olive oil

50g pumpkin seeds, toasted

200g soft, rindless goat's cheese

dressing

75ml extra virgin olive oil

3 tbsp good balsamic vinegar

4 Medjool dates, very finely chopped

½ tsp cayenne pepper (optional)

Sea salt and freshly ground black pepper

Meanwhile, place the cavolo nero onto a large serving platter and drizzle with the oil. Then get your (clean) hands in and massage the leaves for a couple of minutes. This sounds a bit bizarre, but it makes the cavolo nero more tender and easier to eat. Then, add half of the toasted pumpkin seeds and set it aside.

To make the dressing, simply shake all the ingredients together vigorously in a tightly sealed jam jar and set aside until serving.

Once cooked, remove the chicken, carefully open the foil parcel and leave the chicken until cool enough to handle. Then, slice each breast into wide strips and toss through the salad with half of the dressing. Crumble the goat's cheese over the top with the remaining pumpkin seeds. Drizzle over the remaining dressing and serve.

sweet potato, kale and leek bubble and squeak with sage

serves 4

This can be made with whatever you have left over in the kitchen. Sweet potatoes can be substituted with regular potatoes, onions for leeks and the kale/cavolo nero for any firm veg like sprouts. I like to just take what I have and make the best of it. A nice alternative is to swap out 200g of the sweet potatoes for Jerusalem artichokes, which adds a different flavour and a type of fibre called a prebiotic, great for a healthy gut. This dish has got me out of many situations when the fridge is almost empty and there are people waiting for food! Serve with a crispy green salad with balsamic dressing.

600g sweet potatoes (about 2 medium), cut into bite-sized chunks (skin left on if liked)

400g potatoes (about 2 medium), cut into bite-sized chunks

2 tbsp olive oil

1 leek, white and a bit of the light green, finely chopped

2 garlic cloves, finely chopped

150g kale, cavolo nero or cabbage, woody stalks removed, finely shredded

50g Cheddar cheese, grated

3 sage leaves, finely chopped

Good pinch of freshly grated nutmeg

Sea salt and freshly ground black pepper

Bring a medium pan of salted water to the boil and cook the potatoes together for about 10–12 minutes or until tender.

Meanwhile, heat 1 tablespoon of the oil in a 20cm non-stick frying pan on a medium heat and cook the leek for 5 minutes, stirring occasionally, until softened. Add the garlic and cook for 1 minute more. Then add the kale (or cavolo nero or cabbage) and cook for 5 minutes, tossing regularly, until wilted. Remove from the heat.

Once the potatoes are cooked, drain well and return them to the pan. Stir in the cabbage mix along with the cheese, sage, nutmeg and enough salt and pepper, to taste.

Return the frying pan to a low–medium heat and add the remaining tablespoon of oil. Squish the mixture back into the pan and flatten it out evenly. It should be about 4cm thick in the pan. Cook the bubble and squeak very gently for 4–5 minutes until the bottom turns golden and a little crispy. Loosen the sides of the mixture away from the pan edge. Invert a large plate on top of the pan and very carefully turn the whole thing over to release the bubble and squeak. Slide it back into the pan, golden-side up, and cook for a further 4–5 minutes until golden and crispy underneath.

Slide the whole thing out onto a chopping board and cut into quarters. Arrange each one on a serving plate and enjoy at once! Great served with a dollop of Greek yogurt and a sprinkling of pine nuts.

kuku sabzi (spicy herbed frittata)

serves 4

There are a lot of ingredients in this one, I know. But mostly spices, which are often lingering in the cupboard anyway and herbs, which are easy to buy. I was intrigued when I first heard about this dish. A spicy frittata-style dish, traditionally topped with barberries and sometimes eaten for the Persian New Year. I have seen versions made with leek, spinach, potatoes and even just egg whites, but after experimenting with different combinations, I have settled upon this as my take on kuku sabzi. A slice is completely divine served with dollop of Greek yogurt, a scattering of pomegranate seeds and some flatbreads, all popped into a container for lunch. >

Oil, for greasing

75g walnuts, halves or pieces

2 tsp ground cinnamon

1 tsp ground nutmeg

1 tsp ground cardamom

2 tsp ground cumin

2 tsp ground coriander

½ tsp turmeric powder

1 tsp ground rose petals or 2 tsp dried rose petals, ground or chopped to a powder (optional)

8 free-range eggs

3 garlic cloves, very finely chopped

1 bunch of spring onions, finely chopped (white and the light green bit)

Leaves from 1 bunch of fresh coriander, finely chopped

Leaves from 1 bunch of fresh flat-leaf parsley, finely chopped

Fronds from 1 bunch of fresh dill, finely chopped

Good pinch of chilli powder (optional)

Sea salt and freshly ground black pepper

to serve

50g pomegranate seeds (from about ½ small pomegranate)

Flatbreads (optional)

Greek yogurt

Preheat the oven to 200°C (fan 180°C), 400°F, Gas Mark 6.

Grease a 23cm pie dish, round cake tin or springform tin. Line the base and sides with baking parchment and set aside on a baking sheet.

Roughly break up or chop 25g of the walnuts, reserving them for later. Blitz the remaining walnuts in a mini blender to a fine-ish powder. Then tip into a dry frying pan over a medium heat along with the spices and ground rose petals and cook gently for 2–3 minutes. Keep the pan moving from time to time to make sure the mix does not burn. Once you start smelling the aroma of the spices, remove the pan from the heat.

Tip the spice mix into a large jug and add the remaining ingredients, except the yogurt and pomegranate seeds, with some salt and pepper and whisk everything together well. Pour the mixture into the prepared dish or tin and bake in the oven for 15–20 minutes or until just set through to the centre and turned a nice golden brown.

Remove from the oven and leave to cool for 10 minutes or so. Then remove from the tin, discarding the paper or, if using a pie dish, put a large plate upside down on top of the dish and flip the whole thing over so that the plate is the right way up and the dish is upside down. You can either flip it back the other way or keep it upside down, whichever side you think looks best. I tend to like its proper top side to be on top!

Cut into eight wedges, serving two per person with a dollop of Greek yogurt, a scattering of the reserved walnuts and the pomegranate seeds. Serve with some flatbread, if liked, also.

paprika and cumin-spiced prawn lunch box rice salad

serves 4

One for the lunch box! Protein-packed prawns can be pricey, so I often opt for the precooked frozen MSC-certified prawns or even change the prawns for some chicken, which I shred up with a fork for this recipe. This is extra lovely when topped with some fresh mango or avocado, too.

2 tbsp butter

225g brown long-grain or basmati rice

1 red onion, finely chopped

2 large tomatoes, cut into small cubes

3 garlic cloves, finely chopped

1.2 litres chicken or vegetable stock

250g raw, peeled MSC-certified king prawns, or precooked frozen prawns

5 slices of jalapeño pepper (from a jar, look for a sugar-free brand), roughly chopped (optional)

1 tsp paprika

1 tsp ground cumin

1 tsp dried oregano

Leaves from ½ bunch of fresh coriander, finely chopped (optional)

Sea salt and fresh ground black pepper

to serve

1 lemon, cut into 4 wedges

Put 1 tablespoon of the butter in a large sauté pan over a high heat and add the rice. Cook it for about 3–4 minutes, moving it from time to time so that all the rice gets a chance to be in contact with the bottom of the pan. The rice should turn golden brown and a little crispy.

Reduce the heat to medium, add the onion and cook for 2–3 more minutes, stirring the pan from time to time. Add the tomato and garlic and cook for 1 minute. Add the stock (it should come to about 1.5cm above the top of the rice – add a little more if necessary). It's usual to cook rice in water, but stock will make this taste extra nice. Then cook it for as long as it says on the packet.

Five minutes before the rice is ready, put the remaining tablespoon of butter in a medium frying pan over a high heat. Once hot, add the raw or precooked prawns, slices of jalapeno (if using), paprika, cumin and oregano along with a pinch of salt. Cook for a couple of minutes, stirring regularly, until the prawns turn pink and are cooked through (if you are using raw prawns).

Once the rice is ready, drain if necessary. Then add the cooked prawns to it along with the coriander (if using). Season to taste and serve with a lemon wedge.

Add some mango or avocado!

Sichuan bang bang chicken with spicy peanut sauce

serves 4

I first ate this in Australia in the early nineties and the taste has stayed with me for life. The version I had did not have the noodles in it, but was a simple shredded salad. If you are like me, veg and chicken will not fill you up until dinner time so noodles have been added. I wanted to avoid refined flours and sugar in this book so I found some wholewheat noodles in the supermarket and although it is crossing cuisines a little, I also cooked this with gluten-free Japanese soba noodles made from buckwheat, which was really good too. If, after searching the aisles, you cannot find either, then regular egg or rice noodles will also work.

2 large skinless, boneless chicken breasts

2 garlic cloves, peeled and halved

1cm piece of fresh ginger, sliced

1 bay leaf

1 red chilli, deseeded for less heat if liked and roughly chopped or a good pinch of chilli flakes

Put the chicken breasts in a medium pan and cover with cold water. Add the garlic, ginger, bay leaf and chilli, cover with a lid and bring the water to the boil. Then turn down the heat and simmer for 10–12 minutes or until the chicken is cooked all the way through and piping hot.

Meanwhile, place the dressing ingredients in a large bowl, add salt and pepper and set aside.

1 tbsp Sichuan peppercorns, crushed

1 tbsp soy sauce

1 tbsp sesame oil

1 red chilli, deseeded for less heat if liked and finely chopped or 1 tsp chilli flakes

4 tbsp no-added-sugar crunchy peanut butter

1 tbsp sesame seeds, toasted

Salt and freshly ground black pepper

salad

200g medium wholewheat noodles or soba noodles

2 carrots, peeled and cut into thin batons

4 spring onions, cut into long, thin strips

1/3 cucumber, cut into long, thin strips

to serve

Large handful of fresh coriander or basil leaves (optional)

Once the chicken is cooked remove it from the liquid and set it aside to cool down a little. Fish out and discard the garlic, ginger, bay leaf and chilli with a slotted spoon. Add 5 tablespoons of the cooking liquid to the dressing in the bowl and whisk everything together until combined. Top the water up in the pan so there is enough to cook the noodles in. Return to a high heat and bring to the boil. Cook the noodles according to the packet instructions.

Once cool enough to handle, slice the chicken into 1cm pieces or shred it using a fork. Add to the dressing along with the carrot, spring onion and cucumber.

Once cooked, drain the noodles well and rinse them under cold running water to help cool them down a little. Add them to the salad also and toss everything together until evenly coated in the dressing. Divide amongst serving bowls, top with the ripped up coriander or basil leaves, if liked, and serve. >

goat's cheese and courgette salad with toasted pine nuts

serves 4

I started using my spiralizer around a year ago. And my social media feed went mad for it as people asked where I got it from. It is a great tool, as you can use this for vegetables such as courgettes or carrots to make fun salads and pasta dishes in double-quick time. If you do not have a spiralizer, just use a peeler or mandoline to cut the courgettes into strips. This salad is delicious served with the Balsamic Roasted Red Onion Tarte Tatin on page 190.

5 tbsp extra virgin olive oil

2 tbsp balsamic vinegar

½–1 tsp chilli flakes, depending how hot you like it (optional)

4 firm, medium-sized courgettes

200g rindless goat's cheese

Leaves from 1 bunch of fresh basil

75g pine nuts, toasted

Sea salt and freshly ground black pepper

Place the oil, vinegar and chilli flakes, if using, in a really large bowl with some salt and pepper and give them a quick whisk together to combine.

Pass the courgettes through a spiralizer, catching the curls on a large tray as you go. I like to cut the courgettes in half to make them easier to pass through. My spiralizer has a couple of blade choices and I like to use the medium-sized one as I find the thinner strands quickly become soggy in the dressing.

Tip the courgette spirals in on top of the dressing and use a long, sharp knife to slash through them a few times to chop slightly. Break the goat's cheese into bite-sized pieces and add in on top, tear the basil leaves over and add the pine nuts. Gently toss everything together and serve at once.

sesame-crusted tuna steaks with quinoa and mango salad and a ginger soy dressing

serves 4

Do try quinoa (keenwa) if you have not already. This nutty, gluten-free grain is very easy to cook and gives a nice alternative to rice or potatoes.

salad

225g quinoa

150g ripe mango pieces, about 1cm cubed (from 1 small mango)

100g baby spinach leaves, finely sliced

Sea salt and freshly ground black pepper

dressing

5 tbsp extra virgin olive oil or rapeseed oil

3 tbsp apple cider vinegar (or balsamic will also work)

2 tsp gluten-free tamari

2cm piece of fresh ginger, peeled and very finely chopped

Sea salt and freshly ground black pepper

tuna steaks

50g sesame seeds

4 x 200g MSC-certified tuna steaks (about 1.5–2cm thick)

2 tbsp sunflower oil

Sea salt and freshly ground black pepper

Put the quinoa on to cook according to the packet instructions.

To prepare the salad dressing, simply put the ingredients along with a little salt and pepper in a screwtop jar, secure the lid and shake vigorously.

Scatter the sesame seeds on a large plate along with a little salt and a fair amount of pepper and then dip the tuna steaks in so that they are evenly coated all over. Divide the oil between two large frying pans over a medium heat. If you only have one large pan, then cook the tuna in two batches rather than squish all four in and stew them! Cook the tuna steaks for around 2–3 minutes per side for a medium-rare finish. If your steaks are thicker than mine, then this will obviously take a little longer. Remove and set aside.

Once cooked, rinse the quinoa under cold running water and set aside to cool down completely. Once cooled, toss it in a large serving bowl with the mango and spinach and season to taste.

Divide the salad among four serving plates (or in my case, four lunch box containers). Place a piece of fish over each salad and then drizzle over the dressing.

beetroot risotto with feta cheese and mint

mushroom and chestnut Lancashire hotpot
with sweet potatoes and thyme

spaghetti with cavolo nero and cashew nut pesto and tomatoes

sweet potato, cavolo nero and rosemary meatball hash
with poached eggs

kidney bean, lamb and leek shepherd's pie
with a cauliflower and sweet potato topping

pasta with lemony chicken and a kale
and cashew nut pesto

chicken cacciatore with porcini, bay and borlotti

garlic roasted vegetables with flaked almonds and parsley

porcini, shiitake and oyster mushroom pasta
with thyme and sage

portobello and porcini mushroom stovetop lasagne
with puy lentils and sage

sweet potato fish pie with haddock, salmon and dill

turkey meatballs with spaghetti, oregano and fennel

Indian-spiced fish cakes with coconut quinoa and coriander chutney

kiddie roast courgette pizza boats with
oregano and basil

quick creamy 'butter chicken' with cashew nut rice

weekday
dinners

beetroot risotto with feta cheese and mint

serves 4

The beetroot can be raw, peeled, sliced up, seasoned with salt and pepper and then roasted in the oven for about 30 minutes at 200°C (fan 180°C), 400°F, Gas Mark 6 or until tender. Alternatively I have found them in the supermarket ready-cooked but not stored in vinegar. Either way, this beautifully coloured risotto is quick, simple and very, very flavourful. It is really important to use a good-quality fresh stock for a good risotto. This risotto will have a more nutty flavour using the wholesome grain that is barley or short-grain brown rice, and they both come with more fibre and higher levels of vitamins, minerals and phytonutrients. Serve with a handful of rocket with some balsamic dressing on for a bit of extra flavour.

1 tbsp olive oil

1 large red onion, finely chopped

450g cooked beetroot (usually vac-packed, but not the vinegared type)

2 garlic cloves, finely chopped

Leaves from 2 sprigs of rosemary, finely chopped

300g wholegrain barley (not pearl barley) or short-grain brown rice

1 litre of a good liquid chicken or vegetable stock

Sea salt and freshly ground black pepper

to serve

100g feta or goat's cheese

Leaves from ½ bunch of fresh mint

25g pine nuts or walnut pieces, toasted

Heat the oil in a large sauté pan over a low–medium heat. Sauté the onion for about 10 minutes until really soft.

Meanwhile, pop the beetroot in a blender, purée until as smooth as possible and set aside.

Add the garlic and rosemary to the softened onion and cook for 1 minute. Stir in the rice and cook for 1 minute more. Add a quarter of the stock and stir regularly until it has been absorbed by the rice. Then add another quarter of the stock and continue this process until all has been used up and the rice is tender. This will take 20–25 minutes.

Stir in the beetroot and season with salt and pepper, to taste. Warm through for a couple of minutes until piping hot.

Spoon the risotto onto serving plates and crumble over the feta or goat's cheese. Scatter over the mint and pine nuts or walnuts and serve.

mushroom and chestnut Lancashire hotpot with sweet potatoes and thyme

serves 4

Lancashire hotpot is usually made with mutton or lamb and regular potatoes on top, and is baked for a long time with the hope of the lamb becoming succulent and moist and the potatoes slightly soggy underneath and crisp on the top. Enjoy a meat-free Monday with this mushroom variation. I have also swapped in sweet potatoes for added vitamin C and antioxidants. >

mushroom and chestnut Lancashire hotpot with sweet potatoes and thyme
cont.

2 tbsp olive oil

1 large onion, finely diced

600ml vegetable stock

2 tbsp sherry, Marsala, red wine or port (optional)

50g dried porcini mushrooms

3 garlic cloves, finely chopped

Leaves from 2 sprigs of fresh rosemary, finely chopped (to give about 1 tsp)

Leaves from 2 sprigs of fresh thyme (to give about ½ tsp)

2 carrots, cut into thin rounds

3 large portobello mushrooms, halved and then cut into slices in the opposite direction

400g chestnut mushrooms, sliced

1 tsp marmite

100g cooked chestnuts (the type that come in a vac-pac or tin), roughly chopped

100g butter or haricot beans, drained

2 x 250g sweet potatoes, peeled or unpeeled and very finely sliced into rounds

Leaves from ½ bunch of fresh flat-leaf parsley, roughly chopped (optional)

Sea salt and freshly ground black pepper

equipment

4 x 500ml ovenproof dishes (about 13cm wide and 4cm deep)

Heat 1 tablespoon of the oil in a large pan over a low–medium heat and cook the onion for 10 minutes, stirring occasionally, until the onion has softened.

As it is cooking, heat the vegetable stock and your choice of alcohol, if using, in a small pan over a high heat. Once boiling, remove from the heat, add in the porcini mushrooms and leave them to soak.

Preheat the oven to 200°C (fan 180°C), 400°F, Gas Mark 6.

Once the onion is nice and soft, add the garlic, rosemary and thyme and cook for another minute. Add the carrot and portobello and chestnut mushrooms and cook these for 5–7 minutes or until everything begins to soften.

The porcini mushrooms should by now have softened, so drain them through a sieve over a medium bowl or jug to catch the stock. Give the mushrooms a rough chop and add them to the pan along with the stock. Stir in the marmite and pepper (it may not need any salt due to the high salt content of the marmite) and leave this mixture to bubble away for about 10 minutes, adding the chestnuts and beans halfway through.

By this time, the mushroom mixture should look really rich and thick. Divide the mixture among the dishes. Arrange the sweet potato slices in two overlapping layers on top of each one and brush all over with the remaining tablespoon of oil. Cover with foil, arrange on a baking tray and pop into the oven to bake for 45 minutes. Remove the foil for the last 15 minutes to allow the potato to catch some colour.

Once cooked, the potato slices should feel tender when pierced with the point of a sharp knife. Remove from the oven, sprinkle with parsley, if using, and serve.

spaghetti with cavolo nero and cashew nut pesto and tomatoes

serves 4

I am loving the dark green antioxidant, calcium and vitamin C-rich leaves of cavolo nero at the moment and using them a lot in place of kale (which can be used in this recipe if cavolo nero is not easily found at your fingertips). The leaves have a certain nuttiness, which gives them a very rounded flavour, along with the sweet, tangy bitterness of this black cabbage. For extra protein in this dish, finish it with a piece of simple pan-fried salmon on top.

50ml extra virgin olive oil

2 garlic cloves, peeled and left whole

500g cavolo nero, woody stems removed and leaves roughly chopped

400g spaghetti or linguini (preferably wholewheat if you can find it)

25g plain cashew nuts

50g Parmesan, finely grated

50ml vegetable stock

2 large tomatoes, diced

Sea salt and freshly ground black pepper

Heat the oil in a medium pan over a very low heat and cook the garlic for 5–6 minutes, turning the cloves halfway through and shaking the pan from time to time so that they don't burn.

Meanwhile, get a really large pan of salted water on to boil. Once boiling, plunge in the cavolo nero and cook for 2–3 minutes until just tender. Depending on the size of your pan, you may need to do this in two batches. Then, using a slotted spoon or tongs, remove the cavolo nero into a colander and set aside in the sink to let excess water drain off.

Return the cavolo nero cooking water to the boil and add the spaghetti to cook for as long as it says on the packet.

Once the garlic cloves are softened and golden, add the cashew nuts and cook for a further 5 minutes, stirring occasionally, until golden.

Once cool enough to handle, squeeze the excess water from the cavolo nero and add the leaves to a food processor. Add 25g of the Parmesan along with the stock. Once the garlic and cashews have had their time, tip them (and all of the oil from the pan) in as well. Blitz this until as smooth as possible and then season to taste.

Drain the cooked pasta well and return it to the pan. Add the mixture from the processor along with the tomatoes and give everything a good stir together. Divide among four serving plates. Sprinkle over the remaining Parmesan and serve.

sweet potato, cavolo nero and rosemary meatball hash with poached eggs

serves 4

There's no rigid formula to this dish. It is a good recipe guideline to use up whatever you may have in the fridge. The meat can even be omitted altogether and replaced with tempeh or tofu if you fancy a veggie dish, or the sweet potato swapped for regular potato or squash. Spring onions or leeks can take the place of the red onion, while cauliflower, broccoli, cabbage or even shredded Brussels sprouts can easily replace the cavolo nero.

4 medium sweet potatoes (about 300g each), cut into bite-sized cubes (skin on or off)

1 large red onion, cut into wedges

3 tbsp olive oil

300g sausage meat or turkey or chicken mince

6 sage leaves, finely chopped

leaves from 1 sprig of fresh rosemary, finely chopped (about 1 tsp)

75g cavolo nero or kale, woody stems removed, very finely sliced

8 free-range eggs

1 tbsp white wine vinegar

sea salt and freshly ground black pepper

Preheat the oven to 200°C (fan 180°C), 400°F, Gas Mark 6.

Scatter the sweet potato and onion on a large baking tray. Drizzle over 2 tablespoons of the oil and season. Roast for 40 minutes, occasionally tossing them about.

Meanwhile, put the meat of your choice in a bowl. Add the herbs, season well and mix everything together until well combined. With clean, damp hands, shape the mixture into eight even-sized balls (about the size of a golf ball). Pop them on a plate as you go, then cover and chill until you need to cook them.

Once the sweet potatoes have been cooking for about 25 minutes, put a large frying pan with the remaining oil over a medium heat. Cook the meatballs for 6–8 minutes, turning regularly, until golden and almost cooked through. Remove the sweet potatoes from the oven, scatter over the cavolo nero or kale and nestle the meatballs in. Return to bake for the remaining time, until the potatoes are soft and beginning to char, the greens lightly cooked and meatballs cooked through.

Meanwhile, poach the eggs (see page 20). Divide the hash between four plates. Use a slotted spoon to scoop the eggs from the water and arrange two eggs on top of each serving. Serve at once.

kidney bean, lamb and leek shepherd's pie with a cauliflower and sweet potato topping

serves 6

This family favourite still contains meat, but you can swap it out for the same weight of beans, lentils and/or vegetables if you want it meat free. Some of the lamb stock can also be replaced with a good red wine for extra bite. I have hidden some extra vegetables in the topping by using the more flavourful sweet potato for the mash, filled out with cauliflower to make it a slower-energy-releasing dish than if using just sweet potato or regular mash. The mushroom and shallot gravy on page 258 is lovely poured over the top of this, but the shepherd's pie is still great without it.

1 tbsp extra virgin olive oil

1 large leek, trimmed, washed and very finely chopped

1 very large onion, finely chopped

3 carrots, cut into small cubes

2 sticks of celery, cut into cubes

3 garlic cloves, finely chopped

450g lamb mince

4 tbsp balsamic vinegar

1cm piece of fresh ginger, peeled and very finely grated

Leaves from 3 sprigs of fresh rosemary, finely chopped (to give about 2 tsp)

1 tsp paprika

1 tbsp spelt flour

450ml good lamb or beef stock

3 squidges of tomato purée

2 bay leaves

100g oyster and or shiitake mushrooms

2 x 400g tins of kidney beans, drained and rinsed

Salt and freshly ground black pepper

topping

600g sweet potatoes, peeled and cut into bite-sized chunks

400g cauliflower, cut into tiny florets

50g unsalted butter

Large pinch of freshly grated nutmeg

25g Parmesan cheese, finely grated (optional)

Leaves from ½ a bunch of fresh flat-leaf parsley, roughly chopped (optional)

Sea salt and freshly ground black pepper

Heat the oil in a large pan over a low–medium heat and cook the leek, onion, carrot and celery for 8–10 minutes, stirring occasionally, until softened. Then, add the garlic and cook for 1 minute. Next, turn up the heat and add the lamb, balsamic vinegar, ginger, rosemary and paprika. Cook for 2–3 minutes, stirring from time to time so that the lamb does not burn but instead turns from pink to brown. Stir the flour through and then slowly stir in the stock until all is added. Add the tomato purée and bay leaves. Bring to the boil and then reduce to simmer for about 20 minutes for the flavours to develop and the vegetables to become tender. After this has been cooking for 10 minutes, add the mushrooms and stir through.

Preheat the oven to 200°C (fan 180°C), 400°F, Gas Mark 6.

As the filling cooks, make the topping. Pop the sweet potato in the top of a steamer pan and cook for 15 minutes, adding the cauliflower after 5 minutes. If you don't have a steamer, then just cook them in boiling water until tender. In which case, drain them off and place them back in the pan over a low heat for a few minutes to dry them off a bit. Either way, once tender, add the butter, nutmeg and a little salt and pepper to season and toss everything together gently. Set aside, keeping warm.

Once the filling mixture has had its time, carefully stir in the kidney beans and remove from the heat. Tip the filling mixture into a 3 litre ovenproof dish (mine is 20cm x 25cm and 6cm deep), spreading it out evenly. Top with the sweet potato and cauliflower mixture. Sprinkle over the Parmesan evenly, if using, and bake in the oven for 20–25 minutes until golden.

Remove from the oven, sprinkle with the parsley, if using, and serve. >

pasta with
lemony chicken and a kale
and cashew nut pesto

serves 4

I was told that the first three years of a child's life are the most important for developing their long-term eating and taste habits, so I tried to introduce mine to as many varied and healthy foods at possible during that time. My daughter will be the first one to say that she tried different types of pastas and sauces as a child. When she was younger, she would sit at the table with her pasta sauce and wholewheat pasta and eat it all up, until one day she announced that she would not be eating any more wholewheat pasta and please could she have the white pasta stuff, which she had eaten at a friend's house. It is a shame that outside forces sometimes change things, but it is really worth getting them started on the healthier options. I have added the chicken for extra protein, but prawns work equally well. Even without the meaty or fishy part, this dish is totally scrumptious.

pasta

350g wholewheat pasta

chicken

1 tbsp olive oil

3 large chicken breasts, cut into bite-sized chunks

Leaves from 3 sprigs of fresh rosemary, finely chopped (or 2 tsp dried oregano)

Finely grated zest of 1 lemon

Sea salt and freshly ground black pepper

pesto

100g kale, hard stalks removed

1 garlic clove

50g cashew nuts, toasted

25g Parmesan, finely grated

25g fresh vegetable or chicken stock

1 tbsp extra virgin olive oil

Sea salt and freshly ground black pepper

to serve

Leaves from ½ bunch of fresh basil (optional)

Bring a large pan of salted water to the boil and put the pasta on to cook for as long as is recommended on the packet.

As the pasta cooks, heat the oil in a large frying pan over a medium–high heat. Toss the chicken in a medium bowl with the rosemary (or oregano) and salt and pepper. Cook the chicken for about 8 minutes, stirring regularly, until it is golden and completely cooked through.

In the meantime, make the pesto. Whizz all of the ingredients together in a food processor or blender to give a rough paste. Season to taste and set aside.

Once the pasta is cooked, drain it well, return to the pan, cover and keep warm.

Once the chicken is cooked, tip it in on top of the pasta along with the pesto. Add the lemon zest and stir everything together. Check the seasoning and then divide among the serving plates. Garnish with some ripped basil, if you fancy it.

chicken cacciatore with porcini, bay and borlotti

serves 4–6

Every time I buy a tin of chopped tomatoes or some passata, I am underwhelmed by the flavour. The sweetness is lacking and most often the tomatoes are lifeless and flabby. I distinctly remember the tomatoes from my father's greenhouse, which were rich and full and sweet, and I wish I could have tomatoes like those within easy reach every time I need them. To recreate some of that sweetness, without pouring in bags of sugar, I have blitzed up some dates with the tomato sauce. Dates naturally contain sugar, but unlike refined sugar, they are also a good source of fibre, B vitamins and antioxidants, making them a better choice for adding a little sweetness to this punchy, savoury tomato sauce.

2 tbsp butter

1 large onion, roughly chopped

1 handful of porcini mushrooms (about 15g)

2 x 400g tins of chopped tomatoes

Leaves from 3 sprigs of fresh thyme

Leaves from 2 sprigs of fresh rosemary, finely chopped

2 tsp paprika

1 tsp cayenne

3 Medjool dates, de-stoned

1 garlic clove, finely chopped

Heat 1 tablespoon of the butter in a large sauté pan (that has a lid) over a medium–high heat. Add the onion and cook for about 10 minutes, stirring from time to time. The onion should take on a good brown colour, but still retain some of its crunchy texture.

As this cooks, place the porcini mushrooms into a small bowl and pour over enough boiling water to just cover. Leave aside to soak.

Put the chopped tomatoes, thyme, rosemary, paprika, cayenne, dates and a little salt and pepper into a blender or processor and blitz it all together until smooth. Set this aside for a moment.

8 chicken pieces on the bone (e.g. 2 thighs,
2 drumsticks, 2 breasts on the bone, halved)

2 bay leaves

200g chestnut mushrooms, sliced

400g tin of borlotti or cannellini
beans, drained

Handful of pitted olives (about 50g),
halved (optional)

Sea salt and freshly ground black pepper

to serve

Large handful of roughly chopped
fresh flat-leaf parsley

Brown rice, wholemeal pasta or crusty bread

Once the onion is cooked, add the garlic, cook for 1 minute, and then tip onto a plate.

Return the pan to a high heat with the remaining tablespoon of butter. Season the chicken pieces well with salt and some black pepper, then cook them for about 2 minutes per side (taking care not to overcrowd the pan otherwise the chicken will boil and not brown). I usually do this in two batches, placing the chicken on the plate with the onion mix once they are browned.

Once all the chicken is browned, return it to the pan along with the onion and the tomato mixtures and add the bay leaves. Drain the porcini mushrooms well, roughly chop them, and add them also. Pop on a lid and once boiling, reduce the heat to simmer away gently for about 10 minutes (it will need about 25 minutes in total). After this time, stir in the chestnut mushrooms, re-cover and simmer for another 10 minutes. Stir through the beans and olives, if using, and give it a final 5 minutes of simmering.

When cooked, the mushrooms should be soft and the chicken's juices run clear. Season the sauce to taste and serve with a large handful of chopped parsley on top and some brown rice, wholemeal pasta or crusty bread, if liked. >

buy the best-quality
canned tomatoes you
can afford: it makes
all the difference to the
taste of this Italian 'stew'

garlic roasted vegetables with flaked almonds and parsley

serves 4–6

I serve this familiar side dish (with an unfamiliar but tasty twist) with the Mushroom and Chestnut Lancashire Hotpot with Sweet Potatoes and Thyme on page 114.

3 large parsnips, peeled and cut into thick equal-sized sticks (about 2cm thick)

3 large carrots, cut into sticks the same size as the parsnips

5 garlic cloves, peeled and bashed

2 large onions, peeled and quartered with root intact

3 large sages leaves, roughly chopped

1 tbsp olive oil

50g flaked almonds

50g tahini paste

Juice of ½ lemon

1 tbsp date paste, or to taste

Sea salt and freshly ground black pepper

to serve

Leaves from ½ bunch of fresh flat-leaf parsley, finely chopped

Preheat the oven to 200°C (fan 180°C), 400°F, Gas Mark 6.

Place the parsnip, carrot, garlic and onion in a large roasting tray. Scatter over the sage leaves, drizzle over the oil and season with salt and pepper. Toss everything together well and then make sure the veg are spaced in a single layer so that they will brown nicely.

Pop in the oven to roast for 40 minutes, tossing halfway through. Sprinkle over the flaked almonds for the final 10 minutes of cooking.

As the vegetables cook, put the tahini and lemon juice in a small bowl with the date paste, 2–4 tablespoons of cold water and some salt and pepper. Whisk together until smooth and set aside.

Once the vegetables are cooked – they should be tender and beginning to catch colour and the almonds golden brown – remove them from the oven and spoon into a serving bowl or platter. Pour over the tahini dressing, sprinkle over the parsley and serve.

porcini, shiitake and
oyster mushroom
pasta with thyme
and sage

serves 4

I have learnt recently that mushrooms such as oyster and shiitake are what the press like to call 'superfoods'. Well, they feel more like wonderfoods to me. They are packed with antioxidants and have potent immune-boosting properties, so I like to add them to my diet often, especially as the days begin to get shorter and the weather cooler. I realise that shiitake and oyster mushrooms are often not available in all of our supermarkets, however, you can change things up a little and use chestnut mushrooms instead. They don't have quite the same nutritional qualities, but are still very flavourful.

300g wholewheat spaghetti or soba or udon noodles

Handful of dried porcini mushrooms (about 15g)

25g butter

250g shiitake and oyster mushrooms or 250g chestnut mushrooms, thinly sliced

Leaves from 3 sprigs of fresh thyme

5 large sage leaves, thinly sliced

200ml of a good liquid vegetable or chicken stock

50g finely grated Parmesan cheese

Sea salt and freshly ground black pepper

to serve

Handful of fresh flat-leaf parsley leaves, roughly chopped (optional)

Put the pasta or noodles on to cook according to the packet instructions.

Meanwhile, put the porcini mushrooms in a cup or small bowl, pour over enough boiling water to just cover and leave to plump up.

Put the butter in a sauté pan over a medium–high heat and once sizzling, add the chestnut, oyster/ shiitake mushrooms, thyme and sage and cook for 5–6 minutes, stirring occasionally until the mushrooms have softened.

After this time, and once the porcini have plumped up, add them and their soaking liquor to the mushrooms along with the stock. Turn up the heat and let everything bubble away for 5 minutes or so to reduce and make the liquid a little stronger in flavour.

Once the pasta or noodles are cooked, drain well and then pop back into the pan with the lid on to keep warm until needed.

Once the liquor has reduced, tip the pasta or noodles into the pan and add half of the Parmesan. Mix everything together, season to taste, and then serve with a sprinkling of the remaining Parmesan and the parsley on top, if liked. A handful of rocket adds some peppery flavour to this also.

portobello and porcini mushroom stovetop lasagne with puy lentils and sage

serves 4–6

A novel way of making a lasagne. My mother used to be reluctant to switch the oven on every time we needed to cook something for lunch, so I have put this in the book with her wishes in mind. Porcini form the dried mushroom component in the filling (try morels instead, if you can find them – they are some of the tastiest mushrooms on the market, and can usually be found in good delis).

tomato sauce

1 tbsp olive oil

1 large onion, very finely chopped

1 handful of dried porcini mushrooms (about 15g)

2 garlic cloves, very finely chopped

5 sage leaves, finely chopped

½ tsp fennel seeds

Good pinch of freshly grated nutmeg

300g portobello mushrooms, finely sliced

2 x 400g tins of chopped tomatoes

400g tin of puy lentils, drained

1 carrot, very finely diced

Sea salt and freshly ground black pepper

First, prepare the tomato sauce. Heat the oil in a large sauté pan (mine is about 23cm wide) over a low–medium heat and cook the onion for about 10 minutes, stirring occasionally, until really soft. Crunchy onion is nice in some dishes, but I feel it is not quite right for this one.

Meanwhile, put the dried mushrooms in a cup or small bowl and pour over enough boiling water to just cover them. Leave them aside to soften until needed.

Once the onion has softened, add the garlic, sage, fennel seeds and nutmeg and cook through for 1 minute. Then add the portobello mushrooms and cook them down for about 10 minutes, stirring occasionally until softened. About halfway through cooking, lots of liquid will come out of the mushrooms so turn up the heat and let it bubble off until almost gone. This helps intensify the mushroomy flavour.

Meanwhile, mix the ricotta, spinach, Parmesan, egg yolk, nutmeg and salt and pepper in a medium bowl and set aside.

Once the portobello mushrooms are cooked, drain the liquid off the dried mushrooms, roughly chop them and throw them into the mushrooms in the pan. Reduce the heat to medium and add the chopped tomatoes, lentils, carrot and some salt and pepper and leave this to bubble away for 10 minutes or so, stirring from time to time so nothing catches on the bottom of the pan.

As this cooks, bring a large, wide pan of salted water to the boil to par-cook the lasagne sheets and add the oil. Drop five of the lasagne sheets in one by one (to help prevent sticking together) and cook for 3 minutes until floppy, but not entirely cooked through. Carefully remove and lay out in a single layer on a large sheet of parchment paper. Dab them dry with kitchen paper and cover with another layer of parchment paper to prevent them from drying out. Repeat with the second batch of lasagne sheets.

Once the tomato sauce is cooked, remove the pan from the heat and ladle half of it out into a bowl, leaving the remaining mixture in an even layer in the pan. Cover the sauce in the pan with five of the lasagne sheets arranged in a single layer, cutting them to fit where necessary. Spread half of the spinach ricotta mixture evenly over the pasta. Then repeat these layers once more.

Return to a low heat and cover with a lid (if you do not have a lid to fit, then just use a flat baking sheet). Bring to a simmer and then leave to bubble away for about 12–15 minutes, or until the pasta sheets have completely softened (check their tenderness by piercing the point of a knife through the centre). Halfway through the cooking time, scatter the mozzarella pieces and thyme over the top, re-cover and leave to finish cooking.

Once cooked, scatter over the basil leaves and serve. >

white sauce

250g ricotta

100g spinach, roughly chopped

50g Parmesan cheese, finely grated

1 free-range egg yolk

Good pinch of freshly grated nutmeg

Sea salt and freshly ground black pepper

other layers

1 tbsp olive oil

10 regular, gluten-free or wholemeal lasagne sheets

125g ball of full or half-fat mozzarella, drained and torn into small pieces

1 tbsp fresh thyme leaves or 2 tsp dried thyme

Leaves from 1 bunch of fresh basil

sweet potato fish pie
with haddock,
salmon and dill

serves 4

I learnt how to make a fish pie the traditional way, with lots of poaching of fish and boiling of eggs. It's a very satisfying end result, but one that takes so much time. During the six o'clock scramble, when all I really want to do is flop down on the sofa with a large glass of something white and cold, spending hours making dinner for the family is not really on the top of my list. This super-quick fish pie can be made in a heartbeat and you can change up the fish to vary the taste. I hope it will earn a place on your weekly dinner plate.

potato topping

500g sweet potatoes (about 2 medium), peeled and cut into 2cm dice

300g potato (about 1 large), peeled and cut into 2cm dice

25g butter

Good pinch of freshly grated nutmeg

Sea salt and freshly ground black pepper

fish filling

2 tbsp cornflour

300ml semi-skimmed milk

700g MSC-certified fish, skinless, cut into bite-sized chunks (I like to use haddock and salmon)

150g frozen peas

½ bunch of spring onions, sliced

Fronds from ⅓ bunch of fresh dill, finely chopped

100g crème fraîche

Sea salt and freshly ground black pepper

Preheat the oven to 200°C (fan 180°C), 400°F, Gas Mark 6.

Bring a medium pan of salted water to the boil and cook the potatoes together for 10–12 minutes or until tender. Alternatively, steam the potatoes, in which case they tend to take on less water, making for a stiffer, drier (and better) sweet potato mash.

As this cooks, put the cornflour in a wide pan with a little of the milk and stir until dissolved and smooth. Then add the rest of the milk while stirring all the time. Place on a low to medium heat and while continuing to stir all the time, bring to a simmer and cook for a few minutes until slightly thickened. Then add the fish, peas, spring onion and dill and cook gently for about 3 minutes, stirring regularly to prevent it from catching on the bottom. Carefully stir in the crème fraîche and salt and pepper, to taste. Remove from the heat and tip into a 2.5 litre ovenproof dish (mine measures 25cm square and 6cm deep).

Once cooked, drain the potatoes well and tip them back into the pan. Mash until smooth (or use a Mouli grater or potato ricer) with the butter, nutmeg and enough salt and pepper to taste. Place spoonfuls of the mashed potato all over the top of the fish filling and spread it out evenly with a fork. Grate over a little more nutmeg if you fancy it and pop on a baking tray in the oven for about 20 minutes until the top is just catching colour and the fish filling is piping hot. Serve at once.

turkey meatballs with spaghetti, oregano and fennel

serves 4

When writing this book with nutritional help from the Dynamic Duo, who are Aidan and Glen, I learnt that as a nation we eat too much red meat. So in this recipe, I have swapped out the omnipotent beef mince for the lesser-used turkey mince. Turkey mince is not everyone's first choice meat, but we at LP HQ have come to rather like it. It is cheaper than most other minces, can take good strong flavour added to it and it is lean. The other thing is, if you are worried about disapproving comments from turkey-sceptic family members, you never have to actually tell them which meat it is they are eating in the first place! I find this method works every time.

tomato sauce

1 tbsp olive oil or butter

1 large onion, finely chopped

2 garlic cloves, crushed

1 tsp fennel seeds

2 x 400g tins of chopped tomatoes

150ml chicken or beef stock

2 bay leaves

1 Medjool date, very finely chopped

1 tbsp dried oregano

1 tsp paprika (optional)

Sea salt and freshly ground black pepper

turkey meatballs

500g lean minced turkey

1 tbsp dried oregano

1 tbsp sunflower oil

Sea salt and freshly ground black pepper

to serve

300g wholewheat spaghetti

Leaves from ½ bunch of fresh basil

25g Parmesan, finely grated or shaved

First make the sauce. Heat the oil in a medium sauté pan over a medium–high heat. Cook the onion for 5 minutes, stirring occasionally, until softened. Then add the garlic and fennel seeds and cook for another minute, making sure that the garlic does not burn. Next, add the tomatoes, stock, bay leaves, date, oregano, paprika, if using, and salt and pepper. Bring to the boil and then reduce the heat a little to simmer for about 15 minutes until thickened slightly.

To prepare the turkey meatballs, place the turkey mince, oregano and salt and pepper into a medium bowl. Using clean hands, mush it all around until evenly combined and then roll the mixture into twelve equal-sized balls, about 4cm across (or weighing about 40g each). Heat the oil in a large frying pan over a medium heat and cook the meatballs for about 4 minutes, turning regularly, until browned all over. You may need to do this in batches so that the turkey balls brown rather than boil. They won't be cooked through at this point, so don't be tempted to bite into one just yet!

Once the tomato sauce has reduced, nestle the meatballs into the sauce in a single layer. Continue to cook for about 10 minutes, giving everything the occasional careful stir.

Bring a large pan of salted water to the boil and cook the spaghetti according to the packet instructions. Once cooked, drain the pasta well, return to the pan and keep warm.

Once the turkey balls are completely cooked through, tip the mixture into the drained pasta, mixing everything together gently. Season to taste and then divide among the serving plates. Scatter over the basil leaves and Parmesan and serve.

Indian-spiced fish cakes with coconut quinoa and coriander chutney

serves 4

Normally the Indian food I eat is from a takeaway and as with most takeaways, as delicious as they are, I never know exactly what is in them and how good for me they may be. Fish cakes are usually a Thai affair, but I have used Indian flavours along with a coconut quinoa for a twist on the South East Asian staple.

quinoa

250g quinoa

5 tbsp regular or light coconut milk

Sea salt and freshly ground black pepper

coriander chutney

1 bunch of fresh coriander (leaves and stalks)

2 garlic cloves, roughly chopped

1 green chilli, deseeded for less heat if preferred, finely chopped

1cm piece of fresh ginger, peeled

2 tbsp natural yogurt

Juice of 1 lime

Sea salt and freshly ground black pepper

Put the quinoa on to cook according to the packet instructions.

As the quinoa cooks, blitz all of the coriander chutney ingredients (reserving a small handful of coriander leaves for garnishing) together in a food processor until roughly chopped. Season to taste with salt and pepper, cover and set aside in the fridge to allow the flavours to develop.

For the fish cakes, bring a medium pan of salted water to the boil and cook the sweet potato for 10–12 minutes until tender. Alternatively, cook for the same time in a steamer. Bring a wide sauté pan of salted water to a gentle simmer and poach the cod fillets for 6–8 minutes until cooked through. Again, these can be cooked in a steamer pan if preferred (you might even fit both in the steamer tray together if you have one large enough).

fish cakes

600g sweet potato, peeled and cut into large bite-sized chunks

600g MSC-certified cod fillets, skin removed

1 tbsp garam masala

1 tbsp ground coriander

1 tbsp turmeric powder

2 tbsp sunflower oil

1 red onion, finely chopped

3 garlic cloves, finely chopped

1 red chilli, deseeded for less heat if preferred, finely chopped

75g gluten-free flour

½ tsp paprika

Sea salt and freshly ground black pepper

Meanwhile, put the spices into a dry medium frying pan and toast them over a medium heat for a few minutes until they just begin to release their aromas. Add 1 tablespoon of the oil and the onion and cook for 5 minutes until the onion begins to brown but still retains its crunch. Add the garlic, cook for 1 minute more, then remove from the heat.

Once cooked, drain the potato and cod, if necessary. Discard any bones from the fish and tip both into a large bowl. Add the spiced onion mixture along with the chilli and some salt and pepper and gently mix everything together well, leaving a bit of texture rather than making it too puréed. I tried this recipe by pulsing it all together in a blender, but then the fish was a little bit too mushy, so this method works much better. Once cool enough to handle, form the fish cakes into eight even-sized patties. These can be made up to a day ahead to this stage and kept covered in the fridge.

Once the quinoa is cooked, remove from the heat, drain well and return to the pan. Stir in the coconut milk, season to taste, cover and set aside to keep warm.

Toss the flour, paprika and a little salt and pepper together on a plate. Dab one side of each fish cake into the flour to stick, before turning them over to coat the other side. Avoid getting flour up the sides if possible.

Heat the remaining tablespoon of oil in a large frying pan over a medium heat and cook the fish cakes for about 4 minutes on each side until golden brown and piping hot through to the centre.

Serve sitting on a bed of the coconut quinoa with the coriander chutney drizzled over the top and a scattering of the remaining coriander. >

kiddie roast courgette pizza boats with oregano and basil

serves 4

A great dish for the children ... you will also find the adults' forks creeping across to have a bit. I have omitted the omnipresent garlic from these as I know that some children think it tastes a bit 'funny'. Use chopped tomato in place of fresh, or even passata if you have it to hand, and vary the toppings to use up bits and pieces from your fridge such as chicken, butternut squash, peas, etc.

3 large courgettes

2 large tomatoes, cut into small cubes

1 tbsp dried oregano

Good pinch of paprika (optional)

100g Cheddar cheese, grated or feta cheese, crumbled

Leaves from ½ bunch of fresh basil, freshly ripped up

Preheat the oven to 200°C (fan 180°C), 400°F, Gas Mark 6.

Cut the courgettes in half, from end to end. Then, using a small spoon or a melon baller, scoop out some of the flesh down the length of the centre so that the courgettes look like a kind of 'boat'. This flesh is great added to cake mixtures, to add moisture and 'hide the greens', so keep them to do that rather than discard them. Arrange the courgette boats on a baking tray.

Mix together the tomato, oregano and paprika, if using, in a small bowl. Divide the mixture among the courgette boats, then sprinkle over the Cheddar or feta cheese evenly. Pop into the oven to roast for 25–30 minutes or so or until the courgettes become a little tender and the cheese is bubbling and beginning to catch colour. Alternatively, you can pop these under the grill to cook them if you like, but the courgettes will not become as tender.

Once cooked, remove them from the oven, sprinkle over the basil and serve. If you are serving this to little kiddies at a party, then it is nice to chop them up into smaller boats to make it easier for them to eat.

quick creamy
'butter chicken'
with cashew nut rice

serves 4

Chicken tikka masala is one of the nation's favourite foods, but there is another dish that should get more attention. A traditional butter chicken sees the chicken marinated first in yogurt, then cooked in the tandoor, giving smoke to the flavour. I believe the sauce, or 'gravy', is cooked, then cooled and puréed to give a smooth texture. The two are then combined to finish. Of course the dish is traditionally cooked using ghee (like a clarified butter) along with lashings of cream. Greek yogurt has replaced double cream for my lighter version and I have simplified the traditional method to make this a doable dish for a weeknight supper.

rice

| 75g cashew nuts, roughly chopped |
| 250g brown basmati rice |

curry

| 5 cardamom pods |
| 1 tbsp garam masala |
| 2 tsp ground cumin |
| 1-2 tsp chilli powder or chilli flakes, depending how hot you like it |
| 1 tsp turmeric powder |
| 1 tsp ground cinnamon |
| 1 tsp ground coriander |
| 1 tsp fenugreek seeds |
| 1 tsp ground cloves |
| 1 tbsp oil |
| 1 large onion, diced into fairly large chunks |
| 4cm piece of fresh ginger, peeled and finely chopped |
| 4 chicken breasts, cut into bite-sized chunks |
| 2 garlic cloves, finely chopped |
| 200ml passata |
| 2 tbsp tomato purée |
| 200g natural yogurt |
| Handful of fresh coriander leaves or chives, roughly chopped |
| Sea salt and freshly ground black pepper |

Toast the cashew nuts in a dry, small frying pan over a medium heat for 2–3 minutes or until they look nice and toasty and golden brown. Tip them onto a small plate for later.

Slam the cardamom pods open with the side of a large knife and pop them in a large pan with the garam masala, cumin, chilli powder or flakes, turmeric, cinnamon, ground coriander, fenugreek and ground cloves. Toast over a medium heat for a few minutes until you begin to smell the aromas. Then add the oil, onion and ginger and cook for 5 minutes, stirring occasionally, until softened.

Meanwhile, get the rice on to cook according to the packet instructions.

Once the onion has softened, add the chicken and cook for 4–5 minutes, stirring regularly until golden. Next add the garlic and cook for 1 more minute. Stir in the passata and tomato purée, bring to the boil and reduce the heat to simmer for 4–5 minutes until the chicken is completely cooked through.

Once the rice is cooked, drain if need be and return to the pan. Stir in the toasted cashews and set aside for a moment to keep warm.

Remove the sauce from the heat, stir in the yogurt and return it to a very gentle heat for 2–3 minutes. Don't boil it at this stage or the yogurt will curdle and separate. Season to taste and remove from the heat.

Divide the rice among the serving plates, spoon the butter chicken curry over, scatter with coriander leaves or chives and serve.

virgin bloody mary with turmeric
and paprika

cinnamon protein pancakes

pepper and tomato egg cups
with spicy salsa

eggs benedict on sweet potato and rosemary
hash brown rostis with easy hollandaise

huevos rancheros with jalapenos
and garlic

spicy baked eggs with spinach,
mushroom and oregano

smoked haddock kedgeree
with pilau and parsley

lazy brunches

virgin bloody mary
with turmeric
and paprika

serves 6-8

This is a family cookbook and for that reason I have omitted the vodka shots for the recipe.
Served over ice with a big stick of celery this is such a refreshing drink.

1 litre tomato juice, chilled

Juice of 1 lemon

1 tbsp turmeric powder

2 tsp paprika

½–1 tsp cayenne pepper

Good pinch of celery salt

3–4 sticks of celery, halved

Freshly ground black pepper

to serve

Ice (optional)

Put all of the ingredients (except the celery) in a large serving jug and gently whisk together. Season to taste with a little pepper.

Put a stick of celery into each serving glass along with some ice, if using. Pour in the virgin bloody mary and serve.

serve with an ice-cold shot of vodka from the freezer on special occasions!

cinnamon protein pancakes

makes about 8 pancakes

I would eat pancakes every morning if I could. Especially ones containing protein powder. They fill me up until lunch, which is no mean feat. I like to use a protein powder with no dairy in as personal preference. I have found Sunwarrior Protein Vanilla Powder, which I buy on the internet, to be the one with the best taste and the most goodness in. Of course, you can omit the protein powder and just stick with the more familiar ingredients. The oats and eggs (and also the protein powder, if using), mean this dish gives perfect slow-release energy for a balanced breakfast.

80g oats

Pinch of salt (optional)

6 large free-range eggs

2 scoops of protein powder (optional)

4 tsp ground cinnamon

2 tsp ground ginger

2 tbsp date purée paste (see page 46) or
2 Medjool dates, pitted and finely chopped

Oil, for cooking

to serve

Handful of fresh berries
and/or chopped mango

I put my oats in my spice grinder to grind them up, but you can put them in the food processor. Blitz until they are almost like a powder and then tip this into a jug. Add the salt, the eggs and the protein powder, if using, and mix everything together with a fork. I like to beat it hard, but I don't mind if some lumps remain. Add the cinnamon, ginger and dates, mix again, and set aside.

If you are using protein powder your mixture will be thicker and may need a tablespoon of water to make it a little thinner.

Get a frying pan nice and hot and add 1 teaspoon of oil. Once the oil is hot, pour in enough pancake batter to make a pancake about 7–8cm in diameter. You know the pan is hot enough when the pancakes begin to cook straight away and do not continue to

spread in the pan. Repeat with the rest of the mixture, pouring in more pancake batter (leaving a 1cm or 2cm space around the pancakes) until there is no more room left in your pan. I managed to fit in five pancakes in one go.

Then, after about 1 minute, flip the pancakes over using a spatula (the pancakes should look golden brown and toasty if cooked enough) and cook again on the other side for 1 minute. Once cooked remove to the serving plate. Repeat with the rest of the batter.

I like to stack these up on a plate and serve them with a handful of fresh berries. They are equally delicious with other fruits such as mango and caramelised apples and a big dollop of Greek yogurt.

pepper and tomato
egg cups
with spicy salsa

serves 4

So many breakfasts that don't contain cereal seem to contain oats, fruit or eggs. I wanted to find a different way to cook eggs and this is what I came up with. These are fun to make with children as they are so colourful and the kids can get involved in the scooping of the pulp, pouring in of the eggs and hopefully enjoy eating them too!

2 large red peppers

Leaves from a few sprigs of fresh thyme (to give about 2 tsp) or a ½ tsp dried thyme

4 large tomatoes (I like to use beef tomatoes)

8 free-range eggs

½ bunch of chives, finely chopped

50g wild rocket

Sea salt and freshly ground black pepper

salsa

1 spring onion, white and green finely chopped

Large pinch of paprika

Sea salt and freshly ground black pepper

Preheat the oven to 200°C (fan 180°C), 400°F, Gas Mark 6.

Cut the peppers in half down their length and discard the green stalk, white flesh and seeds. Arrange, cut-side up, on a baking tray, scatter half of the thyme leaves over and season with salt and pepper. Pop into the oven to roast for 15 minutes.

Meanwhile, slice about a 1cm top off each of the tomatoes, reserving them for later. Run a small, sharp knife around the inside edge of each tomato to loosen the flesh. Then, using a spoon, scoop the insides out into a sieve set over a bowl and leave to drain really well.

Once the peppers have had their time, remove the tray from the oven and carefully arrange the tomato shells on the tray beside them. Scatter the remaining thyme into them along with a little salt and pepper and return to the oven for 10 minutes.

By this time the peppers and tomatoes should be nicely softened. Remove from the oven, crack an egg into each one and return to bake for 8 minutes.

Meanwhile, chop the reserved tomato tops into small dice and pop them into a medium bowl. Tip the tomato flesh and seeds from the sieve in on top, discarding the juice. Stir in the spring onion and paprika and season to taste with salt and pepper.

Remove the baked vegetables from the oven once the egg whites are set and the yolks set on top, but runny inside. Cook them for a few more minutes if you prefer your yolks hard. Carefully lift a pepper half and tomato onto each serving plate. Scatter over the chives, spoon on the tomato salsa, pile some rocket beside them and serve.

eggs benedict on sweet potato and rosemary hash brown rostis with easy hollandaise

serves 4

If you have a food processor and still have all the attachments stashed away in the cupboard, then now is a good time to get them out. There is a brilliant attachment on my Magimix that grates veg in seconds. It took me a while to find it, dust it off and figure out how to use it, but now I cannot get enough of using this to shred and chop my veg. The other option is, of course, the cheese grater, which is still pretty quick but obviously just needs a bit of elbow grease to get the job done. I have experimented with all kinds of hollandaise substitute recipes using things like Greek yogurt and crème fraîche, but the only way to make a decent hollandaise is by using good, honest butter.

hash brown rostis

2 x 250g sweet potatoes, skin on

3 free-range eggs

Leaves from 3 sprigs of fresh rosemary, finely chopped (about 2 tsp)

2 tbsp extra virgin olive oil

Sea salt and freshly ground black pepper

Preheat the oven to 180°C (fan 160°C), 350°F, Gas Mark 4.

Roughly grate the sweet potatoes and then, picking up handfuls of it, squeeze out any liquid. Another option is to put the grated potato in a clean tea towel and squeeze it like mad. There may not be any liquid in yours, but sometimes I have been known to get a rogue batch of sweet potatoes with excess liquid in. Once as dry as possible, pop the grated potatoes into a large bowl. Beat the eggs to combine and add them along with the rosemary and some salt and pepper and mix together well. >

eggs benedict on
sweet potato
and rosemary
hash brown rostis
with easy hollandaise
cont.

'easy hollandaise'

150g butter

3 egg yolks

15ml lemon juice (from about ½ lemon)

Sea salt and freshly ground black pepper

poached eggs

8 free-range eggs

1 tbsp white wine vinegar

to serve

2 handfuls of baby spinach
leaves (about 50g)

Put two large frying pans over a medium heat and add 1 tablespoon of the oil to each. Divide the potato mix in half and spoon four equal-sized piles of one half into one pan, spaced apart, and then the other half in the same way into the second pan to give eight piles in total. Squish them all down a little with the back of the spoon so each one is about an 8cm wide, flat pancake.

Cook them for about 2–3 minutes on each side or until golden brown and set. Then, carefully lift them onto a large baking sheet and pop into the oven to bake for 10–12 minutes until tender.

Meanwhile, to make the hollandaise, melt the butter in a small pan on the hob or in a bowl in the microwave and remove. Put the egg yolks and lemon juice into a jug blender and blitz for about 30 seconds until just starting to go lighter in colour. Then with the blender still running, slowly add the melted butter through the feeder. Once all the butter is mixed in, turn the blender off. The sauce should be thick, pale and creamy. Pour it into a small pan, season to taste with salt and pepper and keep warm.

Bring a wide sauté pan of salted water to a gentle simmer and add the vinegar. Crack an egg into a ramekin or small jug and carefully pour it into the water. Repeat with the remaining eggs. Leave to cook gently for 3 minutes for a runny yolk (or a minute or two longer if you prefer them hard).

Place two hash brown rostis onto each serving plate. Add half a handful of the spinach leaves and then top with two poached eggs, removing them from the water with a slotted spoon and blotting the base of the spoon on kitchen paper so that the eggs are not too 'wet'. Spoon over the hollandaise and serve immediately.

huevos rancheros with jalapenos and garlic

serves 2

I have had this served with chopped avocado, beans, rice and all sorts, so please do feel free to include one (or all) of those as an accompaniment if you fancy it.

2 soft corn tortillas

2 tbsp olive oil

4 ripe tomatoes, cut into cubes

3 spring onions, finely chopped

2 green jalapeno chillies or ½ regular green or red chilli, deseeded for less heat if preferred, finely chopped

1 garlic clove, finely chopped

Good pinch of ground cumin

Leaves from ½ bunch of fresh coriander, roughly chopped

4 free-range eggs

Sea salt and freshly ground black pepper

Preheat the oven to 200°C (fan 180°C), 400°F, Gas Mark 6.

Wrap the tortillas in a piece of tin foil, sit on a baking sheet and put them in the oven for about 10 minutes or until they are heated through.

Meanwhile, heat 1 tablespoon of oil in a large non-stick frying pan over a medium–high heat. Add the tomato, spring onion, chilli, garlic, cumin and a little salt and pepper and cook them for about 5 minutes or until the tomato begins to break down.

Stir in half of the coriander, remove from the heat and keep warm.

Rinse out and dry the pan and put it back on a low-medium heat. Add the remaining tablespoon of oil and once nice and hot, crack in the eggs, spaced apart. Cook them gently for about 3–4 minutes until the whites are cooked but the yolks still a little runny. Remove the pan from the heat.

Remove the tortillas from the oven and place one on each serving plate. Divide the salsa mix between them, spreading it out with the back of the spoon. Slide two eggs on top of each one, sprinkle with the remaining coriander and serve.

spicy baked eggs with spinach, mushroom and oregano

serves 6

This is based on a family recipe from a friend of my daughter and I added things such as spinach and mushrooms to make it extra filling and to add some more colour. Truly nutritious and exceptionally delicious, this very warming and attractive dish is fast becoming one of my family's favourite brunches. Feta can be added in with this or used to replace the eggs, while tofu or tempeh also work well in place of the eggs.

2 tsp ground cumin

2 tsp paprika

1 tsp cayenne

1 tbsp extra virgin olive oil

1 red onion, halved and then finely sliced

2 tsp dried oregano

2 red peppers, deseeded and cut into thin strips

2 orange peppers, deseeded and cut into thin strips

125g chestnut mushrooms or shitake and oyster mushrooms, finely sliced

1 large garlic clove, finely chopped

2 x 400g tins of chopped tomatoes

1 red chilli, deseeded for less heat if preferred, finely chopped (optional)

80g baby spinach, roughly chopped

6 free-range eggs

Leaves from ½ bunch of fresh flat-leaf parsley, roughly chopped (about 2 tbsp)

Sea salt and freshly ground black pepper

Put the cumin, paprika and cayenne in an ovenproof sauté pan over a gentle heat and cook for 2–3 minutes until you start to smell their aroma. Tip them onto a plate and return the pan to a medium heat.

Add the oil along with the onion and oregano and cook for about 10 minutes until softened, stirring from time to time so that the onion does not catch.

Put the oven on to preheat to 180°C (fan 160°C), 350°F, Gas Mark 4.

Once the onion is ready, add the peppers and mushrooms and cook for another 10 minutes or so until softened. Then add the garlic and cook for 1 minute. Stir in the tomatoes and the chilli, if using. Return the spices to the pan and season to taste with salt and pepper. Bring to the boil and then reduce the heat to simmer for 5 minutes until thickened slightly. Stir in the spinach for a minute or so until wilted and then remove from the heat.

Carefully crack in the eggs in separate spots around the top of the sauce, then place the whole thing in the oven to bake for 10–12 minutes. The whites should be set but the yolks still runny.

Once cooked, remove from the oven, sprinkle with the parsley and serve.

smoked haddock kedgeree with pilau and parsley

serves 4

I was baffled when I first saw kedgeree on the menu for breakfast. I was trying to figure out what place rice and curry powder had on an English breakfast table. Now understanding its Anglo-Indian roots, I welcome this wonderfully flavoured dish to my early morning eats. There is a fair amount of pan juggling, which is why I saved the dish for brunch when there is more time, rather than breakfast. The haddock can be cooked in the microwave, covered with both water and a lid, for about 5–6 minutes to make things a little easier.

300g basmati rice

2 tbsp mild, medium or hot curry powder

400g MSC-certified undyed natural smoked haddock

2 free-range eggs

Bunch of spring onions, finely chopped

Leaves from ½ bunch of fresh flat-leaf parsley, roughly chopped (about 2 tbsp)

Leaves from ½ bunch of fresh coriander, roughly chopped (about 2 tbsp)

Sea salt and freshly ground black pepper

Put the rice on to cook according to the packet instructions, adding the curry powder to the water.

As the rice cooks, place the haddock in a wide sauté pan with the skin side facing upwards so that it is easy to remove once cooked. Cover the fish with boiling water from the kettle and then cover the pan with a lid. Simmer for about 8 minutes or until the fish is completely cooked through.

Meanwhile, place a small pan of water on a high heat and once at a rolling boil, carefully add the eggs. Boil for 6 minutes for a softish yolk or 8 minutes for hard-boiled.

Once cooked, drain the water off the fish. Then once cool enough to handle, carefully peel off and discard the skin, flake the fish into fairly large chunks and keep warm.

Once the rice is cooked, remove from the heat and drain if necessary. Add the flaked fish, spring onion, parsley and half of the coriander and gently stir through. Season to taste with a little salt and pepper.

Once the eggs have had their time, immediately drain them and refresh for a minute in cold water. Peel and halve the eggs.

Divide the rice among four serving plates, sit half an egg on top of each, scatter over the remaining coriander and serve.

roast butternut squash beef 'tacos'
with guacamole lime salsa

tomato chilli mussels with garlic,
basil and thyme

pumpkin and sweet potato gnocchi with sage
and toasted almond flakes

baked chipotle chilli haddock with a red pepper and
red onion relish, and capers

balsamic roasted red onion tarte tatin with tarragon

shaved raw Brussels sprout salad
with hazelnuts, pomegranate and pumpkin seeds

chicken with pineapple and ginger,
and coconut rice

mustard-glazed pork leg escalopes with sweet potato
and apple and toasted flaked almonds

tomato, onion and caper salad with anchovies and basil

pan-fried salmon fillets on herbed lentils
with a winter gremolata

leek, aubergine and chickpea tagine
with cashew nuts and apricots

penne pasta with prawns, scallops and peas

easy spelt pizza with harissa, mozzarella and basil

chicken souvlaki with kale and tomato salad and tzatziki

cooking for friends

roast
butternut squash
beef 'tacos' with
guacamole lime salsa

serves 4

If you are making this one for the
children, a half squash may seem like a
bit too much, so a quarter of one may
fare better. This is delicious with the
guacamole salsa, but a dollop of sour
cream goes great with it too. >

roast butternut
squash beef 'tacos'
with guacamole
lime salsa
cont.

squash

2 small butternut squash

25g butter, cut into small dice

Sea salt and freshly ground black pepper

filling

1 tbsp olive oil or butter

1 large onion, finely chopped

2 garlic cloves, very finely chopped

½ tsp smoked paprika

½ tsp ground cumin

400g lean minced beef

5 tbsp tomato purée

400g tin of chopped tomatoes

100g sweetcorn (frozen and defrosted or drained from a tin)

Sea salt and freshly ground black pepper

guacamole salsa

2 ripe avocados

1 ripe tomato, finely chopped

2 spring onions, trimmed and finely chopped

Juice of 1 lime

Sea salt and freshly ground black pepper

to serve

25g Cheddar cheese, grated (optional)

Handful of fresh coriander leaves (optional)

Preheat the oven to 200°C (fan 180°C), 400°F, Gas Mark 6.

Cut both butternut squash in half from top to tail and scoop out and discard the seeds. Using the tip of a small sharp knife, slash the flesh of each one, cutting about 1cm deep into it. Sit them, cut-side up, on a baking tray, dot the butter over the top and season with salt and pepper. Pop into the oven for 45–50 minutes or until the squash flesh is tender.

As the squash cooks, make the filling. Heat the oil or butter in a large pan over a low–medium heat. Add the onion and cook for 5–6 minutes, stirring occasionally, until just starting to brown. Stir in the garlic, paprika and cumin and cook for 1 minute more. Then increase the heat to high, add the beef and tomato purée and cook for 6–8 minutes until browned, stirring from time to time so that the meat does not catch on the bottom. You may need to use a wooden spoon to bash up the meat a bit to make sure it cooks evenly. Then, add the tomatoes and sweetcorn and cook for 3–4 minutes. Season to taste, remove from the heat and set aside.

Ten minutes before the squash is ready, make the guacamole. Halve the avocados, discard their stones and scoop their flesh out into a medium bowl.
Give it a rough mash with a fork and then stir in the remaining ingredients. Season to taste with salt and pepper, spoon into a serving bowl and set aside.

Once the squash is cooked, remove it from the oven. Arrange a half on each serving plate and spoon the minced beef mixture into the hole of each. Sprinkle over the grated cheese and coriander, if using, then serve with the guacamole and enjoy.

tomato chilli mussels
with garlic, basil
and thyme
serves 4

I know some people are not comfortable with serving mussels at home, but I always say that everyone should try cooking mussels (rich in omega 3 and selenium) at least once as it is strangely satisfying. Scrape off any white barnacles and give open mussels a tap, they should just close slowly. Any which do not close should be discarded. A variation of this would be simply to use some white wine and stock with herbs and garlic.

1 tbsp olive oil or butter

5 shallots, peeled and finely chopped

3 cloves of garlic, finely chopped

1 tsp fennel seeds

1 tsp cayenne

2 x 400g cans chopped tomatoes

1 red chilli, deseeded for less heat if preferred, finely chopped (or ½ tsp dried chilli flakes)

leaves from 4 sprigs of fresh thyme (to give about 1 tbsp)

1–2 tsp maple syrup, optional

1.75 Kg mussels, barnacles removed and any which don't close when tapped discarded

Leaves from 1 bunch of basil

Sea salt and freshly ground black pepper

to serve

Warm crusty bread or wholewheat spaghetti

Heat the oil or butter in a large pan over a low–medium heat. Add the shallots and cook for about 5 minutes, stirring regularly, until softened. Add the garlic, fennel seeds and cayenne and cook for another minute. Then add the tomatoes, chilli, thyme and a little salt and pepper. Turn up the heat, bring to the boil and reduce the heat to simmer away for 10 minutes, for the sauce to thicken and for the flavours to get stronger. Then taste the sauce: if the tomatoes are a little sharp, add the maple syrup a bit at a time to sweeten the sauce to your liking.

Tip in the mussels and cover with a tight-fitting lid. Cook the mussels for 4–5 minutes or until the mussel shells have opened. Then remove from the heat and discard any mussels that have remained closed. Tear half of the basil in, giving it a good stir through to wilt. Season to taste and serve with the remaining basil leaves scattered over the top. Lovely served with some warm crusty bread or wholewheat spaghetti.

pumpkin and sweet potato gnocchi with sage and toasted almond flakes

serves 4

I wrote a cheat's method for gnocchi in my *Fast, Fresh and Easy Food* book. Instead of using the traditional potatoes, I used mascarpone, Parmesan and flour, enveloping them all in a rich pine nut and basil pesto. This dish is superbly tasty, but as the essence of the book is healthy, some minor adaptations have been made to make it thus. The recipe may not be the fastest one in the world, but it's certainly extremely rewarding. And it is not only carrots that help you to see in the dark, sweet potato and pumpkin can both help with your eye health. >

pumpkin and sweet potato gnocchi with sage and toasted almond flakes

cont.

gnocchi

250g sweet potato (a small to medium-sized one)

425g tin of pumpkin purée or 1.2kg butternut squash or pumpkin

1 tbsp olive oil (only if roasting butternut squash or pumpkin)

175g spelt flour, plus extra for dusting

50g grated Parmesan cheese

¼ tsp paprika

Couple of big pinches of freshly grated nutmeg

Sea salt and freshly ground black pepper

for sauce recipe please see overleaf

There are two ways to cook the sweet potato. Either preheat the oven to 200°C (fan 180°C), 400°F, Gas Mark 6. Slice the potato in half from top to tail, place it on a baking tray, season with a little salt and pepper and bake for 40 minutes or so until tender. Or you can prick the potato all over with a fork and microwave it on high for around 10 minutes. Which method do you prefer? I am still clinging on to the oven and roasting them as I think it gives you a slightly sweeter flavour, which naturally I love.

If you are using butternut squash or pumpkin instead of the tinned purée, then cook this in the same way as the sweet potato, but tossed in the oil if oven roasting or adding a little dash of water if microwaving (draining it well once tender in this case).

While the potato (and squash, if using) is cooking, heat the oil for the sauce in a medium sauté pan over a medium heat. Add the shallots and cook for 5 minutes until just beginning to soften. Add the garlic and cook for 1 more minute. Pour in the chopped tomatoes, sage, ginger and cinnamon and season with salt and pepper, then bring to the boil before reducing the heat a little and leaving it to bubble away for about 15 minutes. Remove and set aside. This can be prepared up to a couple of days in advance and kept in the fridge.

Whichever way you chose to cook your sweet potato, squash or pumpkin, once they are cooked, let them cool a little and then peel off the skin. Deseed the squash or pumpkin. Place the sweet potato flesh in a bowl with the tinned pumpkin or 425g of your own cooked squash or pumpkin >

pumpkin and sweet potato gnocchi with sage and toasted almond flakes

cont.

sauce

1 tbsp olive oil

3 shallots, peeled and finely chopped

3 garlic cloves, finely chopped

2 x 400g tins of chopped tomatoes

4 sage leaves, finely chopped

2cm piece of fresh ginger, peeled and finely chopped

½ tsp ground cinnamon

Sea salt and freshly ground black pepper

to serve

25g ready-toasted almond flakes

and mash with a masher until smooth (if you have any squash mash leftover, you could use it in a soup or as a pasta sauce). Alternatively, you could blend them in a food processor or mixer, but they should be soft enough to mash easily by hand.

Add the flour, half of the Parmesan, paprika, nutmeg and salt and pepper. Mix it all together to give a slightly damp and sticky dough. When the dough is the right consistency, you should be able to roll up a small ball with it. If you find the dough is too wet, add a little more flour.

Sprinkle a generous amount of flour on a clean surface and line a large tray with baking parchment. Divide the gnocchi into four equal pieces and roll one out on the floured surface into a sausage about 40cm long and 2.5cm thick. Cut it into 20 x 2cm long pieces, arrange them on the lined tray so they don't touch and cover with a clean tea towel. Repeat with all of the gnocchi mix and then put them in the fridge for about 20 minutes to firm up a little. These can be prepared to this stage a day or two in advance.

When ready to cook, get a really wide, non-stick pan with about 5cm of salted water on to boil. Working in two to three batches, carefully drop the gnocchi in so they form a single layer beside each other in the water and cook for 3–4 minutes. They will rise to the top when ready. Use a slotted spoon to scoop them out and return them to the lined tray until all are cooked.

Meanwhile, get the sauce back on the heat to warm through for a few minutes until piping hot. Slide the cooked gnocchi into the sauce and carefully stir them through to evenly coat. Serve at once, topped with the remaining Parmesan and toasted almond flakes.

baked chipotle chilli haddock with a red pepper and red onion relish, and capers

serves 4

The red pepper and red onion relish in this dish is extremely versatile and goes well with chicken, steak and, of course, fish. If you have the time, double up the ingredients to make a big batch – it will keep in the fridge for about 3 days and can be used to add flavour and boost the healthy nutrient content of many meals, due to the relish being high in antioxidants and vitamin C. Haddock has overtaken cod for me as my white fish of choice as it seems to have more flavour. The date paste is an excellent sweetener to have in the fridge (it will keep for about a week) to slightly sweeten dishes and salad dressings.

2 red peppers, deseeded and cut into strips

2 yellow peppers, deseeded and cut into strips

2 red onions, cut into thin slices

4 MSC-certified haddock fillets (not smoked)

2 tsp chipotle chilli flakes (regular chilli flakes are fine, too)

4 tbsp capers, drained and lightly rinsed

3 tbsp extra virgin olive oil, plus extra for frying

½–1 tbsp date purée paste, or to taste (see page 46) (optional)

Sea salt and freshly ground black pepper

to serve

Watercress (optional)

½ bunch of chopped fresh parsley or 1 handful of ripped-up fresh basil leaves

Preheat the oven to 200°C (fan 180°C), 400°F, Gas Mark 6.

Heat 1 tablespoon of oil in a frying pan, then add the peppers and the onion. Cook for about 20 minutes over a low heat, shaking the pan from time to time so that the vegetables do not burn.

As the pepper mix cooks, place one of haddock fillets onto a square of tin foil, big enough to wrap the fish in. Season the fillet with a tiny bit of salt and some chilli flakes, then wrap up the fish, making a parcel. Repeat with the remaining fillets.

Place the fish parcels onto a baking tray and pop in the oven for around 10–12 minutes, or until the fish is completely cooked.

Once cooked, remove from the oven and set aside for a moment. Tip the peppers into a small bowl, then add the capers, date purée paste (if using) and extra virgin olive oil and mix together. Season to taste (it will probably not need any salt added as the capers are quite salty) then set aside.

I put some watercress down on a plate as a base for my fish, place the fish on top of that and finish by piling the red pepper relish on top. Sprinkle with the parsley or basil, then serve.

balsamic roasted red onion tarte tatin with tarragon

serves 4

I made my first tarte tatin at Leiths School of Food and Wine when I started out as a chef. I loved the magic of the finished product when it was turned upside down to reveal dark golden brown caramelised apples. My second version was one with tomatoes, which looked beautiful when served at the table with the ruby juicy globes. Although this red onion version does not have such a vibrant colour, I believe it surpasses tomatoes on the taste and once cooked, these alliums take on a savoury sweetness that I balanced out with the aniseed hint of tarragon. But please do switch up the herbs with your favourite if tarragon is not the one for you – parsley, basil and even coriander will all work beautifully in this dish. When peeling the onions, I try not to take off too many of the outer layers of the skin as that is where most of the nutritional goodness is.

Knob of unsalted butter

2 pitted Medjool dates, very, very finely chopped or 1 tbsp date paste (see page 46)

6 tbsp of good balsamic vinegar

3 sprigs of fresh thyme

600g red onions, peeled and cut into wedges

Leaves from 1 bunch of fresh tarragon, roughly chopped

Sea salt and freshly ground black pepper

pastry

225g plain or wholemeal spelt flour, plus extra for dusting

75g unsalted butter

1 egg

Pinch of salt

Put the butter in a 20cm non-stick, ovenproof frying pan over a medium heat and allow to melt. Add the dates and cook them down for a moment or two until they start to break down a little. If you are using date paste, then just put it in and stir. There is no need to cook it for a minute or two, just proceed to the next step.

Add the balsamic vinegar and thyme sprigs and continue to cook for a couple of minutes until slightly reduced. Add the onions and cook them for about 10 minutes, stirring frequently, until caramelised.

Meanwhile, preheat the oven to 180°C (fan 160°C), 350°F, Gas Mark 4.

To make the pastry, place all of the ingredients in a food processor and whiz them together until they start to form a smooth ball of dough. If using >

swap the herbs if you're not too fond of the anise hit of tarragon – parsley, basil and coriander make for more than worthy substitutes

balsamic roasted red onion tarte tatin with tarragon
cont.

plain spelt flour, add 3 tablespoons of water to help bring it together. If using wholemeal flour, you will need to add a further 1–2 tablespoons of water.

Alternatively, to make by hand, put the flour and butter into a large bowl. Pick up bits of the mixture with the tips of your fingers and rub your thumb into your fingers to blend the ingredients together, allowing it to fall back into the bowl. Keep doing this until the mixture resembles fine breadcrumbs. Lightly beat the egg in a small bowl and stir into the crumbs really well with a small knife until lumps start to form. Add the water (as above) to bring it together. Lightly dust a clean surface with flour and roll out the pastry to a 20cm circle that is about two-thirds the thickness of a pound coin (about 2mm).

Once cooked, remove the onions from the heat, stir all but a tablespoon of the tarragon through and season with salt and pepper. Use a couple of spoons or forks to carefully turn the shallot halves over so the cut sides are down. Then place the circle of pastry on top, tucking the excess pastry down the sides so everything is nice and snug. Transfer to the oven and cook for 25–30 minutes or until the pastry is cooked through and just turning golden.

Once cooked, remove from the oven and carefully invert onto a plate. Sprinkle with the remaining tarragon and serve. Great with some greens or a crispy salad.

shaved raw Brussels sprout salad with hazelnuts, pomegranate and pumpkin seeds

serves 4-6

There is only one thing which is not quite super easy with this dish and that is the cutting of the nutrient powerhouses that are sprouts. I have recently dusted off my food processor and put one of those attachements on it which usually just stay in the top shelf of the cupboard. However, who would have thunk it but these attachments actually make the whole job so much easier and you can chop the whole lot in a few minutes! If, however, you do not have one of these machines, then put your favourite music on and enjoy slicing your sprouts.

75g pumpkin seeds

500g Brussels sprouts, outer leaves removed

100g roasted hazelnuts, roughly chopped

400g can puy or green lentils, drained (or 250g pack of ready to eat puy lentils)

75g raisins

150g pomegranate seeds (from 1 large pomegranate)

dressing

6 tbsp extra virgin olive oil

3 tbsp balsamic vinegar

Sea salt and freshly ground black pepper

Put a medium frying pan on a medium–high heat and dry fry the pumpkin seeds for 2-3 minutes until toasted and just beginning to pop. Remove and tip onto a small plate to cool.

Mix the dressing ingredients together in a really large bowl and season well with salt and pepper.

Very thinly slice the sprouts by hand (or I like to use the slicing attachment in my food processor for a speedier job).

Toss the sprouts, pumpkin seeds, hazelnuts, lentils, raisins and all but a handful of pomegranate seeds into the dressing, giving it a good mix all together.

Spoon the salad out onto a large serving platter, sprinkle the remaining pomegranate seeds over the top and serve.

chicken with pineapple and ginger, and coconut rice

serves 4

I love sweet-and-sour chicken. It is the stickiness that gets me, and when it came to coming up with a healthy alternative, I became a little stuck. I researched 'refined sugar free' variations and the only ones I could find were laden with artificial sweeteners and, well, that is no good. So I pulled the tastiest bits from my favourite dish – the chicken, the pineapple and the heat – and developed this super-quick version, which I have found family and friends really enjoy, even the little ones!

rice

250g brown rice (or quinoa)

200ml regular or low-fat coconut milk

chicken stir-fry

400g tin of pineapple chunks in natural juice

2 tbsp cornflour

Juice of 1 lime

2 tbsp rice wine vinegar

Cook the rice or quinoa in salted water according to the packet instructions.

Meanwhile, prepare the sauce. Drain the pineapple juice out of the tin into a small jug. Place the cornflour into another small jug, add 4 tablespoons of the pineapple juice and stir together until smooth. To this add the lime juice, rice wine vinegar, tomato purée, soy sauce and five-spice powder. Mix everything together until well combined and set aside.

2 tbsp tomato purée

1 tbsp low-salt soy sauce

½ tsp five-spice powder

2 tbsp sunflower oil

4 skinless, boneless chicken breasts, cut into bite-sized chunks

1 red pepper, deseeded and sliced

125g baby corn, cut into 1cm lengths

3cm piece of fresh ginger, peeled and very finely chopped

4 tbsp chicken stock or water

2 garlic cloves, very finely chopped

1 red chilli, deseeded for less heat if preferred and finely chopped, or 1 tsp chilli flakes (optional)

1 bunch of spring onions, trimmed and sliced

50g cashew nuts, roughly chopped and toasted

to serve

Handful of fresh coriander leaves (optional)

Heat 1 tablespoon of the oil in a large pan or wok over a really high heat. Add the chicken and stir-fry for 5–6 minutes, stirring regularly, until golden all over. Add the remaining pineapple juice and allow it to bubble down to almost nothing, but leaving the chicken coated. Remove from the pan and keep warm.

Wipe the pan out with kitchen paper, add the remaining tablespoon of oil and place over a low–medium heat. Add the red pepper, baby corn and ginger and stir-fry for 2–3 minutes until just beginning to soften. Add the chicken stock or water, garlic and chilli, if using, and cover with a lid. Leave to cook for another 2–3 minutes, giving it a quick stir halfway through.

Finally, remove the lid and return the chicken to the pan along with any juices, the pineapple chunks, spring onion, cashew nuts and reserved sauce. Give everything a good stir up and continue to stir-fry over a gentle heat for 2–3 minutes until the sauce thickens. Remove from the heat.

Once the rice is cooked, drain if necessary and then return to the pan. Add the coconut milk and warm through over a gentle heat for 2–3 minutes.

Divide the rice onto the serving plates and arrange the chicken mixture on top. Scatter the coriander over, if liked, and serve at once. >

mustard-glazed pork leg escalopes with sweet potato and apple and toasted flaked almonds

serves 4

Some people have told me that they eat chicken pretty much every day and that it can get a bit repetitive, so I have included something that I know we as a nation are quite partial to – pork. Not in its usual form of chops, but in its naturally better-for-you form of escalopes. If pork really is not something you want to eat, then do just use a large chicken breast per portion instead.

vegetables

750g sweet potatoes, cut into bite-sized chunks, skin can be left on or taken off

3 large apples, peeled, cored and cut into chunks

25g butter

Good pinch of nutmeg (optional)

Sea salt and freshly ground black pepper

Bring a large pan of salted water to the boil. Add the sweet potato and cook for 3–4 minutes until the chunks begin to have a little give in them. Then add the apple pieces and continue to boil for 6–7 minutes until both are completely tender.

Meanwhile, mix together the mustard, balsamic vinegar, sage, thyme and salt and pepper in a wide, shallow dish. Dip the pork in on both sides to evenly coat in the mixture. Heat the oil in a large frying pan over a medium–high heat and fry the pork escalopes for about 2 minutes on each side until cooked through. >

if you prefer, mash the sweet potato and apple together
instead of leaving them in chunks

mustard-glazed
pork leg escalopes
with sweet potato
and apple and
toasted flaked almonds
cont.

pork

3 tbsp of your favourite mustard (Dijon, wholegrain or I love English mustard)

2 tbsp balsamic vinegar

5 sage leaves, finely chopped

1 tsp fresh thyme leaves or ½ tsp dried thyme

8 pork leg escalopes

1 tbsp sunflower oil

100ml chicken stock or white wine

Sea salt and freshly ground black pepper

to serve

Toasted flaked almonds (optional)

Once tender, drain the potato and apple well and return to the pan. Add the butter, nutmeg (if using) and salt and pepper to taste and then set these aside to keep warm.

Remove the cooked pork escalopes from the pan and add the stock or wine. Reduce the heat and simmer gently for 1–2 minutes to reduce a little and give a flavoursome sauce.

Divide the potato and apple among four serving plates along with two pork escalopes each. Drizzle over the sauce, sprinkle over the flaked almonds, if using, and serve at once.

tomato, onion and caper salad with anchovies and basil

serves 2-4

I love to serve my pasta with garlic bread, but eating one made with spelt would mean making one from scratch and the beauty of pasta is that it is quick, so I feel it needs a quick accompaniment. This colourful and tasty salad can be made with or without the anchovies as I realise they are not everyone's favourite! Capers not only add a flavour balance of acidity to this dish, but they are also packed with antioxidants and have heart-protecting and anti-inflammatory properties.

4 tbsp extra virgin olive oil

2 tbsp balsamic vinegar

400g cherry tomatoes, halved

1 red onion, very finely sliced

50g capers, drained and rinsed

6 anchovy fillets, drained

Leaves from ½ bunch of fresh basil, roughly torn

½-1 tsp chilli flakes, depending on how hot you like it (optional)

Sea salt and freshly ground black pepper

Whisk the oil and vinegar together in a medium bowl until combined. Add the remaining ingredients and toss together gently. Season with a little salt and pepper to taste and serve.

pan-fried salmon fillets
on herbed lentils
with a winter gremolata

serves 4

Trying to save on washing up with this recipe, I have reheated the lentils in the pan in which the fish was cooked, but if you are a microwave lover, then just pop them in there to reheat while you wait for the fish. The gremolatas that I have made in the past have simply consisted of parsley, lemon zest and garlic, which makes for a very summery taste. I threw in some anchovies and kale to give a more wintery tone and it complements the salmon in a wonderfully earthy way. I find it easiest to cook the salmon with the skin on, as it holds the fish together well and then people can choose whether they wish to eat the skin or not. This is a great dish for topping up those healthy essential fats levels, with one serving providing our omega-3 needs for a whole week.

salmon

1 tbsp olive oil

4 x 150–175g MSC-certified wild salmon fillets, skin on

Sea salt and freshly ground black pepper

Get the salmon on to cook. Heat the oil in a large frying pan over a medium heat (a medium heat will preserve the omega-3 levels as very high temperatures tend to destroy them). Dab the salmon fillets dry and season with salt and pepper. Cook skin-side down for about 6 minutes without moving them, until crisp and golden. Then carefully flip them over and cook for 3 or so minutes or until they are just cooked in the middle but still nicely moist and tender. >

pan-fried salmon fillets
on herbed lentils
with a winter gremolata
cont.

gremolata

Leaves from 1 bunch of fresh flat-leaf parsley

100g kale or cavolo nero, woody stems removed

2–4 garlic cloves, depending on how much you like garlic, peeled and roughly chopped

2 tbsp extra virgin olive oil

4 tbsp fish or vegetable stock

1 red chilli, deseeded for less heat if preferred, roughly chopped (optional)

Finely grated zest and juice of ½ a lemon

6 anchovy fillets, drained

Sea salt and freshly ground black pepper

lentils

2 x 400g tins of puy or green lentils, drained

4 tbsp balsamic vinegar

Leaves from 4 sprigs of fresh thyme (to give about 1 tbsp)

Large handful of wild rocket (about 25g)

Sea salt and freshly ground black pepper

Meanwhile, put all of the gremolata ingredients into a food processor and pulse them together to give a rough mixture rather than a purée. Season to taste with salt and pepper and set aside.

Once cooked, remove the salmon fillets on to a plate, cover with foil to keep warm and drain the fat from the pan. Tip in the lentils, balsamic vinegar and thyme with some salt and pepper and cook them over a high heat for 2–3 minutes, stirring from time to time, until warmed through. Stir through the rocket until just wilted and remove from the heat.

Divide the lentils among four serving plates, place a salmon fillet on top of each one and finish with a good serving of the gremolata.

leek, aubergine and chickpea tagine with cashew nuts and apricots

serves 4–6

When I visited Morocco, couscous was the carb of choice to serve with the tagines, which I enjoyed. Couscous is basically like pasta as it is made with wheat flour, which is of course fine to eat from time to time. For a quietly healthier and equally enjoyable alternative, buckwheat works excellently with this rich tagine. Buckwheat is a misnomer as this hardy grain-like pseudocereal is actually gluten free and a member of the rhubarb family. I found it online at three of the five big supermarkets, but if you are not having an easy job of finding it, then use some spelt or brown rice. I have also made this with some MSC-certified cod by covering 4 cod fillets in a pan with fish stock with a bay leaf in, and bringing the stock to the boil. Then turn down the heat and simmer the fish for about 8 minutes, depending on how thick it is. Once the veg is cooked, I just flake the fish into the tagine and serve. >

leek, aubergine
and chickpea tagine
with cashew nuts
and apricots
cont.

tagine

2 tbsp ras el hanout

2 tsp turmeric powder

1 tsp ground cumin

1 tbsp olive oil or butter

2 leeks, outer layer removed, split down the length and finely sliced

3 garlic cloves, finely chopped

2cm piece of fresh ginger, peeled and very finely chopped

2 large aubergines, top and tailed and cut into bite-sized cubes

2 carrots, peeled and thinly sliced

2 x 400g tins of chopped tomatoes

250ml vegetable stock

400g tin of chickpeas, drained

150g cashew nuts (not salted or roasted)

12 dried apricots, roughly chopped

Sea salt and freshly ground black pepper

buckwheat

350g buckwheat

50g harissa paste (look for a sugar-free one)

Leaves from ½ bunch of fresh flat-leaf parsley, roughly chopped (optional)

Freshly ground black pepper

to serve

Leaves from ½ bunch of fresh mint or coriander (optional)

Heat a large pan over a medium heat and add the ras el hanout, turmeric and cumin and allow them to toast for a few minutes until they start to release their aromas. Then add the oil or butter and leek and cook for about 5 minutes, stirring regularly, until the leek softens. Add the garlic and ginger and cook for 1 minute more. Stir in the aubergine, carrot, tomatoes, stock and salt and pepper and increase the heat to bring to the boil. Then, reduce to simmer away for 15 minutes, adding the chickpeas for the last 5 minutes.

As this cooks, put the buckwheat on to cook according to the packet instructions.

Heat a medium frying pan on a medium heat and toast the cashew nuts until golden, tossing regularly. Tip them onto a plate and set aside.

Once the buckwheat is cooked, remove from the heat, drain if necessary and return to the pan. Stir in the harissa and parsley, if using, along with a little pepper and then set aside with the lid on to keep warm.

To check the tagine is ready, the carrot should be tender and the aubergine soft but with a little give in it. Add the apricots and the cashew nuts and gently stir together. Season to taste.

Divide the buckwheat among the serving plates. Ladle the tagine on top, garnish with fresh mint or coriander leaves, if using, and serve.

penne pasta
with prawns, scallops
and peas

serves 4-6

A bit of a luxury supper dish, with sweet prawns and scallops and the delicate taste of aniseed from the fennel. I know some people do not like fennel so you can substitute it for some sliced up onion instead, in which case throw in a handful of coriander or parsley leaves to beef up the flavour.

350g wholewheat pasta

1 tbsp olive oil

1 fennel bulb, very finely sliced, with fronds reserved in cold water

½ tsp fennel seeds

200g raw or cooked prawns

200g raw or cooked scallops

150g frozen peas

2 large tomatoes, cut into bite-sized chunks, or 125g cherry tomatoes, halved

1 tsp chilli flakes (optional)

Handful of rocket leaves (about 25g)

Sea salt and freshly ground black pepper

to serve

1 lemon, cut into wedges

Bring a large pan of salted water to the boil and cook the pasta according to the packet instructions.

Meanwhile, heat the oil in a large sauté pan over a medium heat, add the fennel and fennel seeds and cook for 3–4 minutes, stirring occasionally, until the fennel is tender. Add the prawns, scallops, peas, tomato and chilli flakes, if using. If you are using raw shellfish, cook for 5–6 minutes until the prawns turn pink and both prawns and scallops are cooked through. If using precooked, just cook for 3–4 minutes until the shellfish is piping hot in the middle.

Once the pasta is cooked, reserve about 100ml of the cooking liquid, drain off the rest and return the pasta to the pan.

Tip the shellfish mix into the pasta along with the reserved cooking liquid and the rocket. Season to taste with salt and pepper and toss everything together well.

Serve at once, topped with the drained fennel fronds and with a lemon wedge for squeezing.

easy spelt pizza
with harissa, mozzarella
and basil

serves 2–4

There are many recipes floating around at the moment for pizza made from various different bases.

pizza base

300g wholemeal spelt flour, plus extra for dusting

7g sachet of fast-action dried yeast

1 tsp fine sea salt

Leaves from 1 handful of fresh thyme (about 2 tbsp) or 2 tsp dried oregano

topping

150ml passata

1-2 tsp harrisa paste (depending on how hot you like things)

1 large tomato, cut into bite-sized chunks

2 x 125g balls of low-fat or regular mozzarella, drained

Sea salt and freshly ground black pepper

to serve

Leaves from ½ bunch of fresh basil

Preheat the oven to 240°C (fan 220°C), 475°F, Gas Mark 9.

Toss the flour, yeast and salt together in a large bowl and make a well in the centre. Add 175ml of warm tap water and stir everything together with a wooden spoon until it starts to form a ball. Then get your (clean) hands in and squidge it all together.

Lightly dust a clean surface with flour, tip the dough out and then knead for about 8 minutes until smooth. Flatten the dough out a bit, sprinkle over the thyme leaves and work them into the dough. You may need to do it in two or three batches as there is quite a lot of thyme to get into the dough. Alternatively, knead the dough for 5 minutes in an electric mixer fitted with a dough hook, adding the thyme for the last minute.

Once the thyme is evenly distributed, roll the dough out to a 30cm round that is about 5mm thick. I like to do this on a lightly floured sheet of baking parchment, which I can then simply slide over onto a large baking sheet. If not using parchment, then sprinkle some flour on the baking sheet before sliding the base on. Cover with a clean tea towel for a moment while you get the topping ready.

Mix the passata and harissa together in a small bowl. Remove the tea towel from the pizza and spread this mixture evenly all over the pizza. Scatter over the chopped tomatoes and season with salt and pepper.

Pop the pizza in the oven to cook for about 10 minutes. Remove the pizza from the oven and tear the mozzarella over the top. Return to the oven to cook for a further 5–10 minutes, or until the cheese is bubbling nicely and the pizza base is going crisp.

Once cooked, remove from the oven, scatter over the basil leaves and serve.

chicken souvlaki
with kale and tomato salad
and tzatziki

serves 4

Whenever I see 'leave to marinate' in a recipe, I usually don't cook it, as when searching to make something, I want to cook it there and then. This chicken does well if marinated for a few hours or overnight, but if you want to cook and eat this now, then 10 minutes or so will be better than not marinating it at all! Some say marinating does not penetrate the meat anyway and others swear by it, but for me marinating is something that, when one has the time, is beneficial to add extra flavour to the meat. I serve this either with toasted pitta bread or a warming brown rice pilau.

chicken

4 tbsp extra virgin olive oil

Juice of 1 large lemon

2 garlic cloves, very finely chopped

1 tbsp fresh thyme leaves or
2 tsp dried thyme

1 tsp chilli flakes (optional)

6 chicken breasts, cut into bite-sized chunks

Sea salt and freshly ground black pepper

Mix together the chicken marinade ingredients in a small jug with salt and pepper. Pop the chicken in a medium bowl, pour over the marinade and toss together. Leave to marinate for at least 10 minutes or overnight (in the fridge) if possible.

Next, mix together the tzatziki ingredients (see overleaf) in a small bowl. Season to taste and then cover and pop in the fridge.

Put the sliced kale or cavolo nero (see overleaf) in a large salad bowl and add the oil. Using clean >

tzatziki

150g Greek yogurt

Leaves from ½ bunch of fresh mint,
finely chopped

⅓ cucumber, finely chopped

Juice of ½ lemon

Sea salt and freshly ground black pepper

kale and tomato salad

75g kale or cavolo nero, woody stems
removed and leaves thinly sliced

Drizzle of extra virgin olive oil (about 1 tsp)

1 large ripe tomato, cut into bite-sized chunks

½ small red onion, halved
and very thinly sliced

2 tsp balsamic vinegar

Sea salt and freshly ground black pepper

pitta

4 multiseed, cereal or wholemeal pitta breads

equipment

8 wooden skewers, which have been soaked
in water for 10 minutes or so (or metal
skewers – no need to soak)

hands, massage the oil into the leaves for a minute or so. This tenderises the leaves and makes them even nicer to eat. Toss the tomato, onion and balsamic vinegar through, season to taste and set aside.

Preheat the grill to high. Thread the chicken breast pieces onto each skewer and place them on a grill tray. Grill the chicken for 5–6 minutes on each side, until golden and cooked through. Alternatively, you can cook the skewers on a griddle pan. Remove the skewers onto a plate and cover with tin foil to keep warm. Once the grill (or griddle pan) becomes free, toast the pitta breads for 1–2 minutes on each side until golden and warmed through.

To serve, put a toasted pita bread on a plate with a little of the kale salad and the tzatziki. Lay two chicken skewers on top and serve.

home-made chive
and Parmesan popcorn

baked popcorn chicken with crispy breadcrumbs
and crème fraîche and chive dipping sauce

gluten-free thyme
cheesy pizza bites

rosemary roast chickpeas and almonds
with smoked paprika

spelt and chilli skinny
breadsticks

parsnip crisps with thyme,
salt and mustard

spicy cashew nut chaat

movie nights

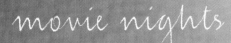
movie nights

parsnip crisps
with thyme, salt
and mustard

p.238

TV snacks, especially those you mindlessly munch in front
of a favourite film, huddled up with your loved ones, are often
of the guilt-inducing variety, but you needn't sacrifice yumminess
by opting for something that's a little healthier. I can guarantee you,
these moreish morsels will disappear well before the credits roll!

spicy
cashew
nut chaat

p 240

gluten-free thyme
cheesy pizza bites

p.232

baked popcorn chicken with crispy breadcrumbs and crème fraîche and chive dipping sauce
p.230

spelt and chilli skinny breadsticks
p.236

rosemary roast chickpeas and almonds with smoked paprika
p.234

home-made chive and Parmesan popcorn
p.228

home-made chive and Parmesan popcorn

serves 2–4

Who would have thought that popcorn is not as bad for us as we had perhaps thought? That stuff at the movies and in the shops, which comes ready-popped or in microwave bags, is not the greatest as it's often full of fat, salt and/or sugar, and it's these processed types that give popcorn a bad name. However, making this classic movie treat at home does make for a better-balanced nibble for you, full of antioxidants. This recipe comes with Parmesan as the main flavour. To try different variations, use paprika, cayenne, curry powder or even things like sesame seeds or cinnamon.

2 tbsp olive oil

100g popcorn kernels

25g Parmesan cheese, finely grated

2 tbsp finely chopped fresh chives or fresh flat-leaf parsley (optional)

Sea salt and freshly ground black pepper

Heat the oil in a really large pan (that has a tight-fitting lid) over a medium–high heat. Add the popcorn kernels, turn down the heat to low–medium and cover with the lid. At first there will be nothing going on as the kernels heat up and get ready to pop. Then, shortly, you will start to hear a few kernels popping before you hear the whole lot join in as they all explode open and hit the top and sides of the pan.

Protecting your hands with oven gloves or a dry tea towel, shake the pan gently from side to side while it is on the hob. This will make sure that all the kernels get the heat!

As the popping begins to slow down, shake the pan a few more times until you are only hearing the odd pop every few seconds. Then remove from the heat, carefully remove the lid and tip the popcorn into a large serving bowl. The whole cooking process shouldn't take more than 2–3 minutes.

Add the Parmesan and herbs, if using, along with some salt and pepper if you think it needs it. Give everything a good toss and serve.

baked popcorn chicken
with crispy breadcrumbs
and crème fraîche
and chive dipping sauce
serves 2-4

Cute little bites of chicken, perfect for a chilled night by the fire in front of the television. Serve with your favourite dip or with this fresh and light crème fraîche one.

breadcrumbs

225g rye or wholemeal bread slices (about 6 small slices)

2 tsp turmeric powder

2 tsp paprika

1 large knob of butter or 1½ tbsp olive oil

Sea salt

chicken

2 free-range eggs

3 large chicken skinless breasts, cut into bite-sized pieces (about 2cm cubes)

Crème fraîche and chive dipping sauce

200g crème fraîche, sour cream or Greek yogurt

Large handful of fresh chives, snipped into small pieces (to give about 3 tbsp)

Juice of ½ lemon

Sea salt and freshly ground black pepper

Preheat the oven to 200°C (fan 180°C), 400°F, Gas Mark 6. Line a large baking tray with baking parchment or a non-stick baking mat.

Break the slices of bread into a food processor, add the turmeric, paprika and a little salt. Blitz to fine crumbs and set aside. Melt the butter or heat the oil in a large frying pan over a medium–high heat and cook the breadcrumbs for 5–6 minutes until they are quite crisp and golden. Then, tip them into a large shallow bowl and set aside until cool.

Crack the eggs into a large shallow bowl and give them a quick beat to combine. Dip the chicken pieces in to coat evenly, allow any excess to drip off, and then toss them in the breadcrumbs until evenly coated. Arrange in a single layer on the baking tray as you go.

Pop the chicken into the oven to bake for 15–20 minutes or until the chicken is cooked through without any pink left inside.

While the chicken is cooking, mix the crème fraîche, sour cream or yogurt and chives together in a small bowl. Add enough lemon juice and salt and pepper to taste. Spoon into a small serving bowl and set aside.

Remove the chicken from the oven, pile it high on a serving plate or bowl and serve with the crème fraîche and chive dipping sauce.

gluten-free thyme cheesy pizza bites

makes 18

If it ain't broke, why fix it, huh? I have been served cauliflower pizza a few times and did not really get it until I was at a friend's and a table of young kids were devouring them as if they were from Pizza Express. I thought what a great way for people to give veg to their kids and so came up with this version, making them into pizza bites rather than a whole pizza. And about the cauliflower. Sshhh, if you don't tell the kids, they will never know!

gluten-free pizza base

1 small cauliflower head, broken into florets
(to give about 500g florets)

1 free-range egg

125g ball of mozzarella, drained and
cut into small dice

25g Parmesan cheese, finely grated

Sea salt and freshly ground black pepper

topping

25g Parmesan cheese, finely grated

25g Cheddar cheese, roughly grated

Leaves from 1 handful of fresh thyme (to give
about 1 tbsp) or 1 tsp dried oregano

Preheat the oven to 200°C (fan 180°C), 400°F, Gas Mark 6. Line a large baking tray with baking parchment and set aside.

Put the cauliflower into a food processor and process it for about 30 seconds until it resembles fine breadcrumbs or rice. Tip this onto the tray and spread it into an even layer. Bake for about 20 minutes, giving it a good stir halfway through. After this time the cauliflower should be a bit steamy and just starting to speckle with colour.

Tip the cauliflower into the centre of a clean tea towel and then draw up the edges to enclose the cauliflower, squeezing hard to release any liquid. Keep squeezing until you get as much liquid out as possible – time to get your frustrations out! There may not be much, but enough to at least dampen the cloth.

Lightly beat the egg for a couple of seconds in a large bowl. Tip the cauliflower 'rice', which by now may be a bit pulpy, in on top. Add the mozzarella, Parmesan and some salt and pepper and mix everything together well.

Tip the mixture back onto the tray and, using clean hands, press and shape it into an 18cm x 23cm rectangle, about 5mm thick, making sure it is nice and level on top. Then bake for 10 minutes until firm, crisp and golden.

Remove from the oven and sprinkle over the topping ingredients evenly. Pop back in the oven for 5 minutes or until the cheese is bubbling. Remove and carefully slide it onto a chopping board. Using a long, sharp knife, cut it in half lengthways and then cut across into 9cm x 2.5cm pieces to give eighteen little sticks in total. Arrange on a large platter and serve.
I tried to serve these as is, without any sauce, but I turned my back for a couple of minutes and lo and behold the ketchup was out!

rosemary roast chickpeas and almonds with smoked paprika

makes 200g

A quick-and-tasty alternative to just plain nuts, which is delicious served straight from the oven. They are pretty firm on the teeth, so easy as you go.

400g tin of chickpeas, drained and rinsed

Leaves from 2 sprigs of fresh rosemary, finely chopped (about 1 tbsp)

2 tsp ground cumin

1 tsp smoked paprika

100g whole almonds

Sea salt and freshly ground black pepper

Preheat the oven to 200°C (fan 180°C), 400°F, Gas Mark 6.

Toss the chickpeas, rosemary, cumin, paprika and some salt and pepper together on a large baking tray. Spread them out in an even layer and bake for 15 minutes until just beginning to crisp up.

After this time, scatter in the almonds and give everything a good toss together. Return to the oven for another 15 minutes until the chickpeas are crisp and have caught colour.

Remove from the oven, tip into a bowl, allow to cool a little and then serve.

spelt and
chilli skinny
breadsticks

makes 28

There is nothing like munching on a crispy something when chilling with friends and family on a lazy Saturday night by the TV. Throw in dried herbs such as dill, thyme or rosemary to make them different each time. I have made them skinny (referring to their shape), but for a fatter breadstick just cut each one to your desired width, then leave them as is or plait or twist them for variation. Serve with your favourite home-made hummus or dip.

275g wholemeal spelt flour, plus extra for dusting

1 tsp fast-action dried yeast

½–1 tsp (depending how much heat you like) chilli flakes

1 tsp fine sea salt

Preheat the oven to 200°C (fan 180°C), 400°F, Gas Mark 6. Sprinkle three large baking sheets with some flour and set aside.

Put the flour, yeast, chilli flakes and salt in a large bowl and toss everything together. Make a hole in the centre of the mix and pour in 225ml warm water. Using a wooden spoon, combine everything well until the mixture starts to come together. Then get your (clean) hands in and squidge it all together to form a ball.

Knead the dough on a lightly floured surface for about 10 minutes if doing by hand, or 5 minutes if using an electric mixer fitted with the dough hook.

Cut the dough in half and leave one half aside, covered with a clean tea towel, so that it does not develop a hard crust. Dust a large square of baking parchment with more flour and roll the dough out to a rectangle about 28cm x 21cm. I like to use the parchment to prevent the dough from sticking to my surface. If the dough is super springy and difficult to roll out, then leave it for a couple of minutes to relax a little. Cut the rectangle into fourteen strips, each about 1.5cm wide. Arrange them spaced apart on the baking sheets. They sometimes get a little floppy and stretch, but that is fine. Repeat with the remaining half of the dough.

You may have to leave one tray aside while you bake the other two, in which case cover with a clean tea towel to avoid drying out. Bake in the oven for 12–15 minutes, swapping the trays around halfway through. Check that any really skinny bits of the breadsticks are not burning, whipping them out if so.

Once cooked, the breadsticks should be crisp and golden brown. They will keep for about a week in an airtight container.

parsnip crisps
with thyme, salt
and mustard

serves 4 as nibbles

I have resisted writing recipes that use a mandoline, the clever little instrument that can cut fruit and veg wafer-thin. My resistance comes from the fact that some of them are not easy to use and often not so cheap to buy. There are some varieties on the market that are excellent, but if a mandoline is not really your thing, then the slicer attachment on your food processor works very efficiently and quickly or even a good vegetable peeler will do the trick.

2 large parsnips

Spray oil

Leaves from 1 large handful of fresh thyme (to give about 2 tbsp)

2 tsp English mustard powder

Sea salt and freshly ground black pepper

Preheat the oven to 150°C (fan 130°C), 300°F, Gas Mark 6. Line two large baking trays with baking parchment or non-stick baking mats.

I tend to wash but not peel the parsnips and then, holding onto their thicker end, use a peeler or mandoline to shave each one into wide strips or ribbons over the baking tray. I find after a while of peeling one side, I need to flip the parsnip over and do the other side. Repeat with the second parsnip, arranging the shavings in a single layer once finished.

Spray some oil evenly over them, sprinkle over the thyme and mustard powder and season with salt and pepper. I like to sprinkle the mustard powder through a fine sieve to prevent it from clumping in one or two areas.

Bake in the oven for 30 minutes, swapping the trays around half way through and giving the parsnips a bit of a toss about before popping them back in. The parsnip strips should be golden brown and crisp once cooked.

Allow to cool a little, adjust the seasoning if necessary, tip into a large bowl and serve.

spicy cashew nut chaat

serves 6

A traditional 'chaat' recipe comes in many forms, but the peanut one I had at an Indian street-food stall in London's East End had ingredients such as dried mango powder and chaat masala, which is a blend of spices. As I struggled to find the exact same ingredients at my local shops in London, I have made a Western version so people can make it in their homes more easily. Nuts in moderation are great as a snack for staving off hunger during the day and apparently are also good to help us have a healthy heart. Serve these cashews divided into little ramekins.

1 tsp ground cumin

½ tsp ground ginger

½ tsp coriander seeds

½ tsp turmeric powder

300g cashew nuts

1 bunch of spring onions, finely chopped

1 large tomato, quartered, seeds discarded and tomato flesh cut into tiny cubes

½–1 tsp (depending how much heat you like) chilli flakes

Leaves from ½ bunch of fresh coriander, finely chopped (about 2 tbsp)

Sea salt and freshly ground black pepper

Heat a small dry pan over a low–medium heat and add the cumin, ginger, coriander seeds and turmeric, and toast for 2–3 minutes, tossing occasionally, until you just begin to smell their aromas. Then tip into a medium bowl.

Now add the cashew nuts to the same pan with a big pinch of salt. Pour in enough cold water to come about 2–3cm over them, pop a lid on and bring to the boil over a high heat. Once bubbling away, take off the lid and turn down the heat to simmer for about 20 minutes, or until the nuts soften. Drain really well and then dab the nuts as dry as possible with kitchen paper.

Add the nuts to the bowl with the spices. Add the spring onion, tomato, chilli flakes and coriander and mix them all together. Season to taste with salt and pepper and serve. I like to divide them into little ramekins and sometimes serve them with a spoon.

mini chestnut, apple
and spinach Wellingtons

easy herby Parmesan roast potatoes

steamed sweet Brussels sprouts
with chestnut, ginger and nutmeg

cranberry, cinnamon and apple sauce

stovetop quick roast carrots

mushroom and shallot gravy

simple roast chicken pieces
with forty cloves of garlic, rosemary and thyme

chermoula roast salmon
with cumin and coriander

Jerusalem artichoke mash

Sunday roasts

a simple Sunday roast

This colourful, vegetarian take on a classic Sunday feast couldn't be easier,
and packs one hell of a punch. I can guarantee you won't miss the meat,
and there's not a nut roast in sight, just full-on flavour and all the goodness of
seasonal vegetables at their best.

**steamed sweet Brussels sprouts
with chestnut, ginger and nutmeg**
p.252

**mushroom
and shallot
gravy**
p.258

mini chestnut, apple and spinach Wellingtons
p.246

easy herby
Parmesan
roast potatoes
p.250

cranberry, cinammon
and apple sauce
p.254

stovetop quick
roast carrots
p.256

mini chestnut, apple and spinach Wellingtons

serves 4

I made beef Wellingtons in *Baking Made Easy* and had not designed another Wellington recipe until this one. These little chestnut and apple ones are quite festive, especially when served with either the Mushroom and Shallot Gravy on page 258 or the Cranberry, Cinnamon and Apple Sauce on page 254, which does make the whole dish quite sweet, but I rather like that in a savoury dish sometimes. The lentils add fibre and some good plant protein, too. I find that potatoes are sometimes too heavy an accompaniment to serve with this, favouring a green salad or green vegetables instead. Use the rich wholemeal shortcrust spelt pastry on page 190 or a ready-made wholemeal pastry.

1 tbsp olive oil

75g peeled and diced butternut squash and/or sweet potato, ready-prepared if preferred

1 small onion, finely chopped

Leaves from 1 sprig of fresh thyme

Flour for dusting

725g rich wholemeal shortcrust spelt pastry (see page 190) or a ready-made wholemeal

1 garlic clove, finely chopped

75g baby spinach

Heat the oil in a large frying pan over a low–medium heat. Add the squash and/or sweet potato, onion and thyme leaves and cook for about 15 minutes, stirring from time to time, until they start to feel tender.

While this is cooking, lightly dust a clean surface with flour and roll out the pastry to about a 36cm square, roughly a quarter of the thickness of a pound coin. Make sure the edges are straight and neat, trimming them with a knife if necessary. Then cut this square into quarters and arrange the four squares on a large baking sheet lined with baking parchment (or double them up with parchment between each pair if the tray isn't large enough). Cover with cling film and refrigerate for about 10 minutes for the pastry to relax and chill.

300g tin of puy or green lentils, drained

75g cooked chestnuts, finely chopped (I found them vac-packed in the shops, but they also come in tins)

25g toasted pine nuts

1 small apple, peeled, cored and very finely diced

Large pinch of freshly grated nutmeg

½ tsp ground cinnamon

½ tsp paprika (optional)

1 egg, beaten

Sea salt and freshly ground black pepper

to serve

Salad leaves

Once the vegetable mix has had its time, add the garlic and cook for a minute more, then tip this into a large bowl. Return the pan to the heat, add half of the spinach along with 1 tablespoon of water and cook this for 1–2 minutes while stirring, until just wilted. Tip into a colander in the sink, then repeat with the remaining half of spinach. Rinse the whole lot under cold water until cool enough to handle, then picking up handfuls at a time, squeeze as much water out of the spinach as possible and add it to the vegetable mixture.

Add the lentils, chestnuts, pine nuts, apple, nutmeg and cinnamon. Add the paprika if you fancy it – I love paprika in pretty much everything. Stir together well and then season to taste with salt and pepper.

Divide the filling mixture evenly among the four squares of now chilled pastry, spooning it into the middle of each. Allow a border of about 2cm around the mixture and paint this border with the egg (reserve the remaining egg). Fold two opposite corners of the pastry inwards to meet each other in the middle. Then fold the other opposite corners into the centre also, but just overlapping the first bit of pastry so they stick securely to form a pouch. Flip them over so the sealed side is down and use a small, sharp knife to slash the tops of the Wellingtons with three 'cuts'. Lay them out in a single layer on the tray and pop them back in the fridge for 10 minutes to firm up.

Preheat the oven to 200°C (fan 180°C), 400°F, Gas Mark 6.

Remove the Wellingtons from the fridge and brush the tops and sides with the remaining egg. Bake in the oven for 25–30 minutes or until the pastry is cooked and golden and the filling is piping hot through to the centre.

Remove from the oven and serve with salad leaves. >

easy herby Parmesan roast potatoes

serves 4

A refreshing change from everyday potatoes for the family. Serve as an accompaniment to the Wellingtons on page 246 or the Chermoula Roast Salmon on page 266.

1kg roasting potatoes, peeled and halved or quartered, depending on size

2 tbsp olive oil

1 tbsp dried oregano

Leaves from 3 sprigs of fresh rosemary, finely chopped

3 tbsp finely grated Parmesan cheese

Sea salt and freshly ground black pepper

Preheat the oven to 200°C (fan 180°C), 400°F, Gas Mark 6.

Bring a large pan of salted water to the boil. Carefully add the potatoes and boil them for 8 minutes.

While they are cooking, drizzle the oil into the base of a shallow roasting tray and place in the oven.

Once the potatoes have had their time, drain them off well and return them to the pan. Shake them to get them nice and fluffy and ensure a crispy finish once roasted.

Remove the roasting tray from the oven and carefully add the potatoes. Season well with salt and pepper and roll them around in the tin so that they are evenly coated in the oil.

Roast for 40 minutes in total. Halfway through, remove them and sprinkle over half of the herbs and Parmesan. Turn the potatoes over and sprinkle the remaining half over evenly.

After 40 minutes, the potatoes should be cooked through, golden brown and really crispy.

steamed sweet Brussels sprouts with chestnut, ginger and nutmeg

serves 4-6

I like to have recipes for Christmas that are cooked on the hob, so I have space in the oven for all the other goodies, and Brussels sprouts are a Christmas classic. Also, cooking vegetables for the shortest time possible means that they will keep more of their bountiful nutrient content. Brussels sprouts are a cruciferous vegetable with a rich content of healthy chemicals called isothiocyanates, which have anti-cancer benefits.

450g small Brussels sprouts

2cm piece of fresh ginger, peeled and finely grated

2 good pinches of freshly grated nutmeg

200g vacuum-packed chestnuts

Knob of butter

2–4 tbsp date purée paste (see page 46)

Sea salt and freshly ground black pepper

to serve

Small bunch of chives, snipped

Steam the Brussels sprouts for about 5 minutes or until the veg are almost tender.

Put a large frying pan over a medium heat and tip in the veg, then add the ginger, nutmeg and chestnuts and cook for 2–3 minutes or until everything is cooked through and the sprouts are tender.

Add the butter and 2–4 tablespoons of the date purée, depending how sweet you want the dish, cook for 1 more minute, and season to taste. Serve with fresh chives sprinkled over the top.

make this sauce ahead of time if you like, and don't forget it's the perfect partner for your Christmas ham, too!

cranberry, cinnamon and apple sauce

makes about 925g

I almost came unstuck keeping with the theme of no refined sugar with this recipe. But trusty dates came to the rescue, giving the sweetness that these tart cranberries so need. This is delicious with turkey and I also serve it with the Mini Chestnut, Apple and Spinach Wellingtons on page 246. It does make the whole dish rather sweet, which is lovely once in a while.

300g cranberries

2 Granny Smith apples, peeled, cored and cut into small cubes

175g pitted Medjool dates, finely chopped

2 tsp ground cinnamon

Finely grated zest and juice of 2 oranges

2 tbsp balsamic vinegar

100ml water

Sea salt and freshly ground black pepper

Stir all of the ingredients, including some salt and pepper, together in a medium pan over a medium-high heat and bring to the boil.

Reduce the heat to simmer for about 10 minutes, stirring occasionally, until the cranberries have burst and softened and the apples and dates cooked down to give a chunky sauce.

Remove from the heat and serve warm or cold. This will keep in an airtight container in the fridge for up to a month.

stovetop quick roast carrots

serves 4

These are a great addition to your roasting repertoire,
especially when the oven is full of other things and there
is no room to cook these lovely orange veg.

Good drizzle of olive oil

Handful of chopped fresh rosemary

750g baby carrots or regular carrots, cut into
6–7cm long and thumb thickness pieces

30g butter

Handful of fresh thyme leaves

Salt and freshly ground black pepper

Put a large frying pan over a medium heat. Add a good drizzle of oil, rosemary and the carrots and season them well. Cook the carrots, keeping them moving around from time to time, for about 7 minutes. Then add the butter and thyme and cook them for another 8–10 minutes or until they are tender. Once the carrots are cooked, season to taste, remove them from the pan and serve.

mushroom
and shallot
gravy

makes 700ml

I know how much children like to eat things with gravy, so it is always good to have a big batch of this on hand. It will keep in the fridge for about 3 days and always comes in handy to pour over things like shepherd's pie or anything that needs a bit of sauce. I have used part chestnut mushrooms and part shiitake mushrooms as shiitake are good at keeping colds and other nasties at bay. The sweet shallots are a prebiotic, which helps promote friendly gut bacteria. So all in all, a pretty good-for-you gravy!

50g butter

200g chestnut mushrooms, quartered or sliced

200g shiitake mushrooms, quartered or sliced

2 shallots (or ½ an onion), finely chopped

Leaves from 2 sprigs of fresh rosemary, finely chopped (to give about 1 tsp) or 1 tsp dried rosemary

3 large sage leaves, finely chopped

50g spelt flour

600ml of a good vegetable, beef or lamb stock

1 tsp Marmite

Couple of glugs of balsamic vinegar (about 1 tbsp)

Leaves from ½ bunch of fresh flat-leaf parsley, roughly chopped (optional)

Freshly ground black pepper

Melt the butter in a medium pan over medium heat. Once sizzling, add the mushrooms, shallots, rosemary and sage and cook them for 10–15 minutes or until the water (that comes out of the mushrooms) has evaporated and the vegetables softened.

Mix in the flour well, and then gradually, while stirring all the time, add the stock. Adding it gradually will help avoid any lumps. If you find you do have some lumps once all of the liquid has been added, then simply whisk it like mad until smooth. Add the Marmite and balsamic vinegar and then leave this to simmer for about 5 minutes, stirring it from time to time, until thickened. Stir the parsley through, if using, and season with pepper to taste (it will probably already be salty due to the marmite content) and then serve. Alternatively, cool completely and refrigerate until needed.

simple roast chicken pieces with forty cloves of garlic, rosemary and thyme

serves 4

Forty cloves of garlic, I know … huge right? I first heard about this dish from my teacher at Leiths School of Food and Wine and rushed home to make it straight away. It is so simple and so delicious, but possibly not one to eat the day before a close liaison with someone new! Garlic has long been heralded for its nutritional properties, but there is a catch to making sure we get them. The garlic needs to be crushed or bashed a little bit to activate its antioxidant, immune-regulating and healthy heart-boosting benefits. Then the garlic needs to be left for about 10 minutes for everything to get activated before you can go ahead and use the cloves for the recipe. Who would have thought it! Removing the papery skin is easy. Just bash each clove with the end of a knife and it comes off very easily. I believe the original recipe uses vermouth or white wine, but I have substituted that for a chicken stock, which is naturally sugar-free. Please try not to use stock cubes or gel, which need to be reconstituted. These normally contain massive amounts of salt and very little true chicken flavour. >

simple roast chicken pieces
with forty cloves of garlic,
rosemary and thyme
cont.

12 chicken pieces on the bone (drumsticks, thighs or halved breasts), skin removed

2 red onions, quartered

40 garlic cloves, peeled and bashed

1 tbsp olive oil

Leaves from 3 sprigs of fresh rosemary, finely chopped (to give about 2 tsp)

Leaves from 4 sprigs of fresh thyme, finely chopped (to give about 1 tsp)

250ml of a good liquid chicken stock

Handful of fresh flat-leaf parsley leaves

Sea salt and freshly ground black pepper

Preheat the oven to as high as it will go (mine goes to 260°C (fan 240°C), 500°F, Gas Mark 10).

Arrange the chicken pieces, red onion wedges and garlic in a single layer in a large ovenproof dish or roasting tray. Drizzle over the oil and scatter with salt and pepper before tossing everything well to coat evenly. Roast in the oven for about 10 minutes until the chicken begins to turn light brown and the garlic catches colour.

Remove the tray from the oven and reduce the temperature to 220°C (fan 200°C), 425°F, Gas Mark 7 (leaving the door open for a minute will obviously help the temperature to drop quickly). Scatter over the rosemary and thyme and pour over the stock. Return to the oven for 20–25 minutes or until the chicken is cooked through.

Once the chicken is cooked (the juices will run clear when the thickest part is pierced with a knife) transfer them to a plate, covering them to keep warm. Then pour everything else from the dish or tray into a blender or processor and blitz it all together for a minute or so until as smooth as possible, giving you a great sauce. Add the parsley (and any juices from the resting chicken) and blitz again. Check seasoning and adjust if necessary.

I like to serve the chicken on a large serving plate with the garlicky sauce in a gravy boat, green vegetables and jacket potatoes or boiled new potatoes with a drizzle of extra virgin olive oil.

chermoula roast salmon with cumin and coriander

serves 4

I know the first time I saw a whole roast fish, I wanted to run a mile. It was all tails and fins and eyes staring at me, and I really did not want to eat it. I am all for the kiddies learning about different cuisines and having culinary adventures tasting different foods, but serving a whole fish, eyes and all, at a family gathering just has not worked for me. So this is a quick and easy roast, using salmon fillets rather than the whole fish. This dish goes beautifully with the Quinoa with Raisins, Walnuts and Parsley on page 88.

2 tsp ground cumin

2 tsp paprika (optional)

2 tsp ground cinnamon

1 tsp ground coriander

1 tsp turmeric powder

Leaves from 1 bunch of fresh flat-leaf parsley

Leaves from 1 bunch of fresh coriander

2–3 garlic cloves, depending on how garlicky
you like it, roughly chopped

Juice of 1 lemon

50ml extra virgin olive oil

4 x 175g MSC-certified salmon fillets, skin on

Sea salt and freshly ground black pepper

Put the cumin, paprika (if using), cinnamon, coriander and turmeric into a dry medium frying pan over a medium heat. Toast the spices for 2–3 minutes, shaking the pan now again so nothing burns, until you just start to smell the aroma of the spices.

Tip the spices into a food processor with the parsley, all but a small handful of coriander leaves, the garlic, lemon juice, olive oil and salt and pepper. Pulse it several times, scraping down the sides occasionally, to give a rough but slightly wet paste. Tip this into a baking dish that will comfortably fit the four salmon fillets.

Place the salmon fillets on top of the chermoula and toss them all around carefully until evenly coated. Leave the fillets skin-side down, cover with cling film and then pop into the fridge for 1 hour (or overnight) to marinate. If you are serving this with the quinoa, then make the quinoa now.

Just before the fish is ready to cook, preheat the oven to 180°C (fan 160°C), 350°F, Gas Mark 4.

Pop the baking dish of fish and marinade into the oven and roast for 15–20 minutes, depending on the thickness of your salmon, or until your salmon is cooked just the way you like it.

Once cooked, remove from the oven and serve garnished with the reserved coriander leaves.

chermoula is a heady, spicy North African spice mix that pairs beautifully with fish

Jerusalem artichoke mash

serves 4

This is one of those lesser known vegetables that I used to glance at while pushing my trolley towards the sweet potatoes in the supermarket veggie aisle. I have now learned that these tubers have much more flavour than I could have imagined, are creamy in texture and the little nutrient-rich powerhouses are full of antioxidants, immune-boosting properties, potassium, iron, copper and B vitamins. In this form they have a slower energy release than mashed potatoes and so will keep your family fuller for longer. They also contain a prebiotic fibre that is great for bolstering good gut bacteria AND even helps us absorb minerals from our diet that keep our bones strong. It would be great to see more of this little wonder-food on menus and in meals! After peeling they do tend to discolour quickly, so squeeze a tiny amount of lemon over them to prevent this from happening, if you are not using them straight away.

800g Jerusalem artichokes, peeled and cut into large bite-sized chunks

30g butter

Pinch of freshly grated nutmeg (optional)

Sea salt and freshly ground black pepper

Put a pan of water on to boil with a little salt in it. Carefully lower the veg into the water and boil them for about 15 minutes (check them after 10) until they are tender. Once cooked, drain them well, add the butter, nutmeg, if using, and salt and pepper, mash with a potato masher and serve.

no-cook chocolate espresso
cheesecake squares

mixed berry crumble
with oats and almonds

sticky peanut butter
and chocolate slabs

how-easy-is-this banana
ice cream

chocolate, banana and ginger
super-quick mousse

tasty chocolate brownies

fruity berry tarts
with vanilla cashew cream

raw vegan moist carrot cake with cashew,
walnut and orange frosting

hazelnut 'ella' chocolate ice cream
(with a touch of coconut)

no-bake chocolate brownies

sweet endings

no-cook
chocolate espresso
cheesecake squares

makes 16

A really quick-and-easy cheesecake using a version of my quick chocolate mousse as a filling. I have used almonds as the nut, but pecans, walnuts or macadamia nuts will work well, too. This does require an hour of freezer time plus 20 minutes resting once out, but it makes a great dinner party dessert or treat-time snack.

Olive oil, for greasing

base

100g whole blanched almonds

25g unsweetened cocoa powder

150g Medjool dates, pitted

Seeds of 1 vanilla pod

filling

3 ripe avocadoes, peeled and de-stoned

3 ripe bananas, peeled and roughly broken up

350g Medjool dates, pitted

100g unsweetened cocoa powder

2 tbsp instant coffee powder or granules dissolved in 2 tbsp of boiling water

Good pinch of fine sea salt

to serve

200g raspberries (optional)

Grease and line an 18cm square tin (at least 5cm deep) with baking parchment, making sure that some excess hangs over the edges. This gives you something to pull on when you want to remove the cheesecake from the tin.

Blitz together the base ingredients in a food processor until they form crumbs that stick together when squeezed. Tip this mixture into the prepared baking tin and, using (clean) hands, press it evenly all over the base. Then pop in the fridge while you make the filling.

Blitz together all of the filling ingredients in a food processor until as smooth as possible. Tip this mixture onto the base, smoothing it out on top with the back of a spoon so it is nice and level. Then put into the freezer for up to 1 hour until firm.

After this time, remove the cheesecake from the freezer and lift it out of the tin. Peel the paper from the sides. Dip a long, sharp knife into a jug of recently boiled water, wipe dry with kitchen paper and cut the cheesecake into sixteen squares, dipping and drying the knife between each cut. Plate up and leave at room temperature for 10–20 minutes to slightly soften and become not so freezer cold.

Arrange the raspberries on top, if using, and serve. Any leftovers can be kept in the fridge and are best eaten within 24 hours otherwise the bananas start to 'turn' and go past their peak, so eating these as soon as possible after making them is best.

mixed berry crumble with oats and almonds

serves 4-6

Making a better-for-you crumble was a challenge. The *Baking Made Easy* in me just wanted to use lots and lots of butter, flour and the like. I played around with the topping a bit, using things like coconut oil and other butter alternatives, but I settled on butter for the best overall flavour and mouthfeel. I felt that the coconut took over the whole thing and masked the flavour of the fruit, but have a go with both and see which one you prefer. This ticks all the boxes for a healthy dessert. The mixture of oats, almonds, berries, dates and cinnamon creates the perfect sustained energy-releasing treat, that packs a hefty nutritional punch.

filling

600g fresh berries

2 Medjool dates, pitted and very finely chopped

1 tsp ground cinnamon

½ tsp ground nutmeg

crumble

180g porridge oats

80g ground almonds

7 Medjool dates, pitted and very finely chopped

4 tbsp butter

3 tsp ground ginger

Seeds of ½ a vanilla pod

Preheat the oven to 190°C (fan 170°C), 375°F, Gas Mark 5.

Put the filling ingredients into a pan over a low heat and cook for about 4 minutes or until the fruit just begins to soften. Tip the fruit into an ovenproof dish and set this aside.

Put the porridge oats, ground almonds, dates, butter, 2 teaspoons of the ground ginger and the vanilla seeds into a bowl and, using your fingertips, rub this gently together to just combine so everything is evenly mixed in. Tip the crumble topping over the fruit and then sprinkle over the remaining 1 teaspoon of ground ginger.

Pop into the oven and cook for about 25 minutes or until the crumble is just going golden brown. Once cooked, remove from the oven and leave to cool for a few minutes before serving. >

sticky peanut butter and chocolate slabs

makes 16

There are lots of peanut butters on the market now that do not have added sugar in them, so have a good scour of the shelves to find the right one. You may find that when you open these kinds of peanut butters, there is some oil on the top. This is totally natural and just needs to be stirred in to combine and then used as normal. Sometimes peanuts and peanut butter get a bad rap, but the good news is peanuts deliver similar health benefits to many other nuts, which is a good excuse to include them in your diet as an occasional healthy snack. Sprinkle the top with some flaked coconut to serve if you fancy it.

Grease and line the base and sides of an 18cm square tin with baking parchment, leaving excess paper hanging over the edges, and set aside.

Place the base ingredients in a food processor and blitz until they stick together when squeezed. Press this mixture into the base of the tin and pop into the fridge for 15 minutes (or freezer for about half that time) to set a little firmer.

Give the processor bowl a quick wipe out and then blitz together the dates and oats for the filling to give rough crumbs. Add the peanut butter, almond milk and vanilla seeds and blitz again until well combined to give a thick, moist paste.

Once the oat base has set, remove from the fridge or freezer and tip the filling mixture on top. Using the back of a spoon or small step palette knife, smooth the filling out evenly. Pop back into the fridge to set for 15 minutes (or again half that time in the freezer).

Meanwhile, put the coconut oil in a small pan over a low heat or small bowl in the microwave to melt. Remove and stir in the cocoa powder until dissolved. Clean the processor bowl out once again and blitz the dates until as smooth as possible. Add the cocoa mixture and blitz again to combine. Leave aside to cool until ready to use.

Once set, remove the slab from the fridge or freezer and pour the chocolate topping all over it. Spread it out evenly with the back of a spoon or small step palette knife and return to the fridge for at least 30 minutes or the freezer for 15 minutes.

Once completely set, remove from the fridge or freezer and use the paper to lift the slab out of the tin. Using a long, sharp knife, cut the slab into sixteen even-sized pieces and serve.

These will keep layered between pieces of baking parchment in an airtight container in the fridge for a few days.

base
150g oats

175g Medjool dates, pitted

filling
125g Medjool dates, pitted

200g oats

450g peanut butter (no added sugar)

50ml unsweetened almond milk

Seeds from 1 vanilla pod

topping
75g coconut oil

4 tbsp unsweetened cocoa powder

50g Medjool dates, pitted

how-easy-is-this
banana ice cream

serves 4

This is like a foodie miracle. I had this on holiday, but using mangoes, then I tried it at home using up some bananas and I was more blown away than I have been with most things that I have made. The simplicity of making something so tasty and requiring the minimal amount of effort really is something else. And as long as you like bananas, you will love this extremely easy snack. The bananas need to be frozen for about 2–3 hours, but then the next step takes seconds.

6 large, ripe bananas

to serve

4 tsp chopped toasted hazelnuts, pecan nuts or almonds (optional)

Good pinch of ground cinnamon (optional)

Small handful of fresh mint leaves (optional)

Peel the bananas and cut them into 2cm thick slices. Tip them into a plastic container (suitable for the freezer), secure the lid on and pop into the freezer for 3–4 hours until just firm.

Once the bananas are frozen, empty them into a food processor and whiz them for a good few moments. The bananas start banging around the food processor at first and things do not look so promising, but gradually they will start to turn into a smooth but thick banana cream. A smooth banana ice cream!

Scoop into four serving bowls, sprinkle with some toasted nuts, cinnamon and/or mint, if liked, and serve immediately.

chocolate, banana
and ginger
super-quick mousse

makes 6 (small portions)

Yes, I know this is a little strange seeing avocado in a mousse recipe. Apple sauce, bananas and things like avocados have been used for some time in sweet recipes to replace butter and other fats. Also, coconut oil is the cooking king at the moment when it comes to all things healthy and raw. However, much as I love the taste of coconut, I find that if used again and again in dishes to replace butter and other fats, the flavour is all-encompassing and very overpowering. For this reason, I have not added coconut oil to my recipes unless I want it to be head of the table. I hope you like the balance of flavours in this familiar, yet unfamiliar chocolate dessert. I love this as a treat for special occasions only, as it does have a high natural sugar content in the dates and bananas. Better for you than usual sugar, but sugary nonetheless (but super yummy)!

2 ripe bananas, peeled and broken into pieces

2 ripe avocados, peeled and de-stoned

125g Medjool dates, pitted

75g unsweetened cocoa powder

2 tsp ground ginger

2 tsp very finely grated fresh ginger

Put all the ingredients into a food processor and blitz together to give a thick and smooth mousse.

Divide the mixture evenly into six small ramekins or bowls to serve for a filling and luxurious mini treat or dessert.

They can be eaten straight away or, for a slightly firmer set, refrigerate for about 1 hour. They are best eaten within 24 hours of making as the bananas start to turn after that time.

tasty chocolate brownies

makes 9

In *Baking Made Easy* I made brownies all singing and dancing with oreo cookies on top. In this healthier book, I wanted to have some brownies with massive flavour, but with a slightly healthier edge. I have replaced the sugar with dates, giving some extra fibre to the mix that will help lessen those sugar spikes. I experimented with avocado in place of butter, which works in some uncooked dishes, but I found that when cooked the avocado flavour was a bit too strong and so kept the butter in. The oats replace wheat flour, giving a more nutritious eat and extra fibre.

Rapeseed oil, for greasing

75g oats

200g Medjool dates, pitted

125g unsalted butter, melted

75g unsweetened cocoa powder

75ml unsweetened almond milk

2 free-range eggs

1 tsp baking powder

Seeds from 1 vanilla pod

Preheat the oven to 180°C (fan 160°C), 350°F, Gas Mark 4. Grease and line an 18cm square baking tin with baking parchment and set aside.

Put the oats in a food processor and blitz until they become like a powder or fine flour. Add the dates, butter, cocoa powder, almond milk, eggs, baking powder and vanilla seeds and process until the mixture is smooth and fudgy.

Spoon the brownie mixture into the baking tin, smoothing the top evenly with the back of a spoon. Bake in the oven for 12–15 minutes until firm on top but a little soft in the centre. That should mean that the centre of the brownies should still be the tiniest bit gooey.

Once cooked, remove from the oven and leave to cool a little. Then, cut into nine squares and serve.

*these are delicious served with my
banana ice cream on page 280*

fruity berry tarts
with vanilla
cashew cream

makes 4

So many people have said to me that when they see a recipe that needs to be started off a little bit in advance, they do not go ahead and make that recipe. So I wanted to give you options here. Ideally the cashew nuts in the filling would love to be soaked for 4 hours or so in water, but if you are a last-minute Larry like I can be so often, then just put the cashews into a bowl, pour over some boiling water to cover them and leave them to sit for an hour instead. Once the cashews have been soaked and have begun to soften, then just drain them completely and set aside while you get on with the rest of the recipe. Berries are such a great source of nutrients called polyphenols, which make them and the foods they are mixed with a lovely slow energy releaser, perfect to avoid those unwanted energy highs and then lows after eating refined sugar. These tarts are wonderful for when you are entertaining guests and need an easy and cool-looking dessert.

Rapeseed oil, for greasing

crust

125g Medjool dates, pitted

250g pecan nuts

filling

150g plain cashew nuts, soaked (see intro)

50g Medjool dates, pitted

Seeds from 1 vanilla pod

fruit

Large handful of blueberries (about 50g)

Large handful of raspberries (about 50g)

Large handful of blackberries (about 50g)

to serve

Leaves from ½ bunch of fresh mint or basil

Grease four x 13cm individual loose-bottomed, fluted or straight-sided tart tins and set aside on a tray.

Place the dates and pecans for the crust in a food processor or mini blender and blitz until they start to clump together. Divide this mixture equally among the tins. Press the mixture onto the base and up the sides of each one, making sure it is of even thickness. Place in the fridge to set for 30 minutes while you get on with the rest of the recipe.

Place the soaked and drained cashews, the dates and vanilla seeds in a food processor or mini blender along with 100ml of cold water. Blend until as smooth as possible to give a creamy mixture.

Once the tart bases have set and are feeling firm, remove them from the fridge and divide the cashew cream among them. Spread it out evenly with the back of the spoon. Top with the berries and then scatter over the mint or basil to serve.

raw vegan moist carrot cake with cashew, walnut and orange frosting

serves 9

Is it low in fat? No, not so much. Is it high in good fats? … Yes absolutely.
It's also refined-sugar free, refined-flour free and vegan!

cashew, walnut and orange frosting

200g cashew nuts

140ml unsweetened almond milk

4 Medjool dates, pitted

Seeds of ½ vanilla pod

carrot cake

300g oats

320g carrots

180g Medjool dates, pitted

50g almonds

2–3 tsp ground cinnamon

1 tsp ground ginger

⅓ tsp freshly grated nutmeg

Handful of walnuts, bashed up a bit

Grated zest of ½ orange

First, start with the cashew nuts. Pop them in a jug, pour boiling water over them and let them sit for about 1 hour minimum and overnight maximum. As I suffer from extreme impatience, I soaked them for 45 minutes precisely and they were good, but the longer the better. Some of them will bob to the top, but that is okay.

While your cashew nuts are bobbing and soaking, make the cake base. Put the oats, carrots, dates, almonds, cinnamon, ginger and nutmeg in a food processor and blitz until they are totally combined. My mixture was a big ball of mush – and that is the right consistency. As this is blitzing, line a 20cm square tin with baking parchment so that it overlaps the sides of the tin. Plonk your mixture into it, then flatten it down using either the back of a large spoon or an offset spatula to make it level, flat and even.

Drain the cashews well, then put them into a blender or NutriBullet. Pour in the almond milk and add the dates and vanilla and then blitz it until it is smooth and creamy. It will have flecks of brown in it (dates) and black (vanilla) and may even have a greyish tinge, but that's all good and it's all very tasty.

Smooth the frosting out on top of the carrot cake with the spatula or spoon so it is nice and flat and about 1cm thick. Sprinkle over the walnuts and the orange zest and pop it in the freezer for about an hour.

Once the carrot cake has been in the freezer for about an hour, pull it out. The frosting should not be frozen or the base, but it will make it easier to cut after its hour-long sabbatical in the freezer.

Cut the carrot cake into sixteen equal squares. Then take lots of pictures of them for your social media posts before tucking into them with bountiful glee.

hazelnut 'ella'
chocolate ice cream
(with a touch of coconut)

makes 1.3 litres

A play on words referring to my daughter's love of that chocolate hazelnut spread that most of us have in the cupboard. Try as I might to get her to eat the wholegrains and greens, fish and lean meat with me, which she does from time to time, that red and white tub with the brown contents always screams to her from the cupboard shelf. So to give my little one something a bit different, with maybe a bit more of the good stuff in, I developed this recipe just for her and I hope you enjoy it too. I have made this with whole hazelnuts, which I bake in the oven for 8–10 minutes at 200°C (fan 180°C), 400°F, Gas Mark 6, tip into a towel and rub them like mad to get the skins off, then chop up in the food processor. I have also made it with the very convenient ready-chopped and roasted hazelnuts, which I found in the supermarket. The recipe requires the mixture to be placed in the freezer for 6–8 hours and whisked up every 30 minutes of the last 3 hours for a lovely ice cream.

2 x 400g tins regular or low-fat coconut milk
200ml unsweetened almond milk
75g unsweetened cocoa powder
200g Medjool dates, pitted
Seeds from 1 vanilla pod
100g chopped roasted hazelnuts (see intro)

Place all of the ingredients except the hazelnuts in a food processor and blitz well until as smooth as possible. It should give a lovely glossy, chocolatey mixture.

Tip this into a 1.5 litre freezer-safe plastic container (that has a lid) and stir in the hazelnuts. Spread out fairly evenly with the back of a spoon. Pop the lid on securely and place in the freezer for at least 6–8 hours.

After 3 hours, give the mixture a good beat up with a fork, especially around the edges and base where it hardens first. Return to the freezer, but repeat this process every 30 minutes until the ice cream is almost set hard. The regular mixing will help prevent big ice crystals from forming, which would not be nice when you come to eat the ice cream. Whisking it every 30 minutes is essential to give you a smoother, creamier feel when you eat it.

The ice cream is ready when it is finally frozen, but much smoother thanks to your whisking! Allow the ice cream to sit out at room temperature for 15–20 minutes before serving so it is scoopable.

no-bake chocolate brownies

makes 16

What could be easier than a brownie recipe that does not even have to be cooked? These are full of healthy fats and contain no gluten or dairy. For me, they can stand shoulder to shoulder with the cooked variety and I think they taste SO good. I shared them with some of my daughter's friends, who at first where not one hundred per cent welcoming of the idea of a raw brownie, but then they soon fell in love at first bite.

Rapeseed oil, for greasing

125g ground almonds

100g pecan nuts, plus 16 for decoration

75g unsweetened cocoa powder

125g dates, pitted

175g Medjool dates, pitted

Grease and line an 18cm square baking tin or dish with baking parchment and set aside.

Place all of the ingredients, except the 16 pecan nuts for decoration, in a food processor. Blitz everything together until it forms crumbs, which if you squeeze together will hold and stick. Then tip this mixture into the tin and level it out evenly using the back of a spoon or a small, step palette knife.

Once flat, mark out sixteen even-sized square portions with the tip of a sharp knife. Press a pecan nut firmly into the centre of each square to decorate. Then pop in the fridge for 15 minutes or so to set.

Once set (it will still be fairly pliable, but it should be set enough for it to be cut), remove from the tin, cut into the sixteen marked-out squares and serve.

These brownies will keep layered between baking parchment in an airtight container in the fridge for a couple of weeks.

Here's to Health

Behind the scenes...

Watson!!

Recipe writing a la pyjamas today x

index

index

index

index

Thank you to everyone who has motivated, supported and inspired me over the years, and specifically on this book.